Ladybird, collected

Ladybird, Collected

told by Meg Heriford

© 2020 by Meghan Heriford
All Rights Reserved

Photos from author's personal collection.
Cover art by Cristie Gunn.

First paperback edition published October 2020.

ISBN 978-0-578-75896-1 (pbk. : alk. paper)

Printed in the United States of America

The paper used in this publication is acid free and meets the minimum requirements of the American National Standard for Permanence of Paper for Printed Library Materials Z39.48-1992.

Many thanks to the Ladybird staff and guests who allowed me to tell their stories in this collection; to Channon and Erin for keeping me in orbit; to the community of Lawrence, Kansas, for your incredible generosity in supplying donations that have served thousands of meals at a crucial time. We will keep going.

And to Arthur Dodge for unpacking his bag all those years ago.

Table of Contents

Foreword

First there was pie. The diner was born of and bloomed around pie. Bakers gathered around the big wood block table in the tiny bakery downstairs, where they rolled and crimped and baked thousands of pies. Crowds streamed in, then flowed back out each day. Recipes were written and refined. Money changed hands. Pie held a steady gravitational pull in the center, keeping us on course and anchoring the exchanges.

At some point, very quietly, the orbit inverted, turned itself inside out. I can't point to where that happened; I only know that one day pie was just flying around with the rest of us as we hemmed a core of community and human interaction.

When I skirted closest to it I began to pluck—with no regularity—moments from the center, shiny nuggets to look at more closely and reassemble into a broader context. Many of those took place at the diner; others are from my life outside of it, which is tethered to this place like a moon. I couldn't have known what I was saving them for, or that one day a pandemic would halt the swirl; freeze these little time capsules in place for me to collect, compile, and sell to hustle funds for a community kitchen.

Here we are.

The dining room is dark for now and the big wood block table is dormant. A new pattern of exchange has emerged. Upon collection and arrangement, the snapshots of who we were and what we've become form a strange arc, really just a beginning and a middle. I'm sorry to say that there isn't much resolution waiting at the end of this book.

The book itself is the means to its own ending.

Spin Again, a Dedication

Nine years. That's how long Carl says he's been on the street, off and on. Mostly on, I surmise. He uses the word chaotic to describe trying to find a safe place to be, somewhere he won't be in danger or worse, mistaken as dangerous. The shelter is full. He stays on the move. Sometimes

I see him every day for a week or so, then maybe not at all for several months. It is always, *always* a relief when he walks in the door. I lay on my best mom guilt and he jokes out an apology about forgetting to call. Sometimes he orders seconds when he finishes his breakfast, or sits a while reading the trivia cards I keep on the tables. He watches the people and the plates go by. He welcomes a conversation if I have time for one, but never demands it of me. His voice is gentle, quiet enough that I slide into the booth across from him and lean in to hear him better. He asks if I need help with anything today. He always asks that. He says he would like to do volunteer work for me and I take a quick mental inventory of my repair list, which today includes rehabilitating a century-old steel counter stool, doing something about the busted tiles in the entryway, and fixing the oven door. I imagine the two of us watching instructional YouTube videos, trying to figure out how to weld and lay tile. What could go wrong? He tells me he has a hard time staying sober. I scratch welding from the list.

I've never seen him drunk and it registers that those are the stretches when I don't see him at all. He says that he should tell me more often how much he appreciates me, says "you are really a lot" and my heart sinks, just drops right onto the table. He is gracious and lovely every time he comes in, but I have not been a lot, haven't been nearly enough, haven't taken any risks for him, or allowed our friendship to evolve beyond being someone he comes to for a meal and a place to wash up. I am someone he only shows the un-messiest parts of himself to. Every time he asks to help me I wave it off as unnecessary but I realize that hidden within that altruistic gesture is a fear that something will go wrong and our friendship will become complicated. The feeling I have when he shows up after a months-long absence, that wash of ease, *there you are, my friend. . . .* I've been selfish with that feeling, and cowardly. If I can't risk my own comfort, I am not the friend I pretend to be, and nowhere near being *a lot*.

Nine years. He's been out there nine years.

I invite him to come on Monday and Thursday mornings to help me load in the deliveries. It's my very least favorite part of this job and I always welcome extra hands to pull in and stock the heavy cases of food. He sometimes brings his laundry with him to wash in the basement machine. He says he's going to try to get back to Kansas City, says there are more and better resources there for him; things like food and shelter are easier to access. He would like a home there someday.

That was early March 2020. I promised him we'd be right here if he made it back this way. I thought I was telling him the truth. Add it to the list of promises I couldn't make good on:

that my kids could play with their grandmother before they knew it; that my daughter would attend a prom and a commencement sometime this summer; that I would have jobs for my staff in a month or so. Every hopeful workaround, every flick of the spinner since March has landed on spin again, spin again, spin again.

This book is dedicated to Carl and in memory of a season of unkept promises, and to the one promise I've honored. I promised at the outset of our closure that we'd do as much as we could for as long as we could in the way of offering food assistance to our neighbors who need it. What I have left to fund those meals are the stories of what we were and what we've become. These are stories from the intersection of commerce and community, which is a busy, sometimes messy place. What follows are snapshots from the swirl of exchange that happens here. I've done my best to capture it with some clarity, to sharpen the blur of things that won't hold still, and to provide a glimpse into the community that has shaped the enormous life of a tiny diner in the middle of the country.

Place

I was born here, although for years when anyone asked how I liked living in Kansas I'd shrug and offer that it's as good a place as any. I'd explain that I don't seem to be someone for whom contentment is contingent on any particular locale. I've lived as happily in the Sonoran desert as I have on the beach as I have tucked into a small valley in the Flint Hills. The only place I couldn't seem to hack it was during the late '90s, in a small city in northwest Pennsylvania where I never did shake the chill from the lake effect. I could not fathom that a cloud cover might maintain outright jurisdiction over a place so completely as to not allow more than a scant glimmer of direct UV rays from October to April. I chased the sun back to the coast of Southern California with little more than a few boxes of books in my trunk and a tragically optimistic philodendron in the passenger's seat of my Volkswagen.

By the time my path wound back to Kansas I wasn't traveling so lightly, with a baby and a husband who had never set foot east of the Gila National Forest. I cheerfully championed the abandonment of temperate weather with assurances of gentle thunderstorms outside screened-in porches, piles of leaves from golden oaks and bright red maples, snow angels, the impetuously early skyward probes of a daffodil. It hadn't been a week since we'd arrived that April when an F4 tornado tore through a town just a couple hours west, making national headlines and exposing the fraudulence of my claims. "Well," I waved off his dubious eyebrows, "it's as good a place as any . . . and look! No scorpions in the sink!" For years I sold myself this bill. Any place is as good as another so long as one has access to a decent cheese selection.

What I underestimated in those younger years is my connection to this place, undeniable as a belly button, that would plunge roots deeper than I'd known I was capable of.

What began to stir in me on the prairie, soaring its terraces and diving into its valleys, felt like being tucked in. The swell of joy was the same as when I'd bounced in the back of my dad's truck as a kid, all the way to Brick's for a milkshake. Tall grass and sunflowers brushed our outstretched hands when he swerved onto the shoulder to make us laugh. Patience earns rewards here. I learned to be very, very still at Carnahan Creek because that's how you'll find frogs and turtles and newts. Days stretched out like the wide sky over hills that look like a thousand napping Bona Deae. This is the womb. Every step I took away from this place was a circle back. To watch my mom walk a trail through the Flint Hills with my kids puts me smack in the middle of the infinite loop, feeling the coming and going of time and blood as sure as the wind on my face. I know that I'm lucky to have it, this connection to a place. I am of this place. "Maybe you are too," I tell my kids. "Travel," I say. "Explore. Have adventures. It's a long life but it's a big world, so don't dally. Go all the way to the moon if you like, but remember this place. And if this doesn't do it for you, don't stop until you find a place that whispers its secrets to you, somewhere the song sings itself."

It's my wish for everyone that they find their soul mate in a salty wave or a foggy marsh or a city corner or a Bluestem hilltop. I'm lucky enough to have been born in my place. It was gifted to me, this recognition, and it ensures that in this often disregarded flyover state I see a wild place, an adventurous place, sturdy geologic treasures and fragile ecological exchanges, but mostly I just feel home. It is where I found my heart, and a place big enough to hold it.

Foundation

I didn't grow up with much conversation on poverty. I was well into my 20s before it occurred to me that powdered milk and economy-sized bags of knock off brand cereal had probably not been my mom's first choice at the market; that her ability to turn anything into creamed something-or-other on toast (pound of hamburger, 6 hard boiled eggs, once even a can of black olives!) for dinner was not the extent of her culinary capability, but was necessitated by a lack of resources as my dad put his history degree to use in a forklift at the steel & pipe supply.

By the time I realized that we'd been poor, we weren't anymore. My parents had access to all the rungs of mobility the American Dream suggests. They were healthy, intelligent, able-bodied, college educated, had a solid network of friends, family and community support, no mental illness, and they had each other. It would be years before I began to comprehend the fortune I was born into, powdered milk and all.

When I was thirteen we rode that American Dream to the land of real milk and honey, right up to its shoreline. There I saw down-and-out right out in the open for the first time. I guess probably my response to seeing people who were unsheltered was some degree of pity. I had no reference point and no preparation for people without shoes talking to themselves in the midst of all that sunshine and wealth. I certainly didn't wonder why or how they ended up without access to food and housing. I did not see addiction, mental illness, domestic violence, restricted access to services, generational poverty or any of the other disparities that destabilize entire families, entire communities. I wasn't heartless, but I wasn't inquisitive either. I came awfully close to being one of those *toss a can of soup in the bin at Christmastime and call it good* types.

The first time I gave a sandwich to someone who asked me for something to eat was also the first and only time I performed the Heimlich maneuver. He was too intoxicated to eat. He began to choke. I always think of him when I hear the expression ‘kill them with kindness’ because that is actually possible to do. For days my whole body was sore from the effort of holding him up, thrusting my fists into his abdomen. I screamed myself hoarse while people in nice clothes looked on. No one helped me. No one helped me help him. He did smell terrible and he did vomit quite a lot once I’d dislodged the sandwich but what is the value of a life? More or less than a Fendi suit? Whatever, I was in an apron anyway.

The sandwich, though well intended, was not helpful, and my takeaway from the whole thing was that I should either stay out of the way or learn to really see people. I chose the latter, not because I’m a good person but because the first option sounded impossible.

I have lots of chances to see people now. Mostly I try to see what's true in people and love them for that, even when it's a little messy. It's not hard to love people in dirty clothes or people who say things you can't make sense of or people who don't have any money. My kids smell bad and say weird stuff all the time. They are also flat broke.

The man who often sits on the bench near the diner is tall and tan, with the sandy look that I associate with those guys who went on ski trips twice a year and ignored me in high school. Sometimes he stretches out his long legs and reclines on his pack, watches the sky or the people go by. He likes to be outside. Actually, he has to be outside. He can't *do* inside. Once he gave my daughters a gift card to McDonalds and told them to go get some ice cream. Someone with great intentions gave him that gift card but he can't go into McDonalds. Can't do inside. For years, no matter the season, my invitations to come in and warm up or cool off have been politely declined. He's tried a couple of times but he just can't sit inside for long. Conversations with him on the bench have revealed small details of a wife and mornings once spent with her in the coffee shop up the block, a normal life. Then the walls constricted and he couldn't *do* inside anymore. So now he's outside. "All year," he says proudly with his knockout smile.

After five years of invitations and a number of false starts, he made it happen one Tuesday just before close. He set his stuff on a table near the door and I tried not to geek out but I think I sort of did. "You're in! What's the occasion?" French fries. He wanted french fries and chili. I fluttered around like a nervous grandmother and Becca teared up a little when I explained his situation and that we shouldn't get our hopes up, that last time he was out the door before his food was ready. But he stayed. He stayed and said that it was the best chili and french fries he'd had in a long time and do we have chef salads? I told him we don't, but we can figure that out next time because although I know outside is where he feels most comfortable and I don't doubt his ruggedness, I do worry that lots of the things he might need access to happen inside, things like medical or psychological services, a dentist . . . inside things. If a chef salad makes the walls expand a bit it is no trouble. After all, what is the value of a life? More or less than a salad?

Root

"Well, we met at a dinner party," the woman explained to the guests seated with her at the table. The meal was finished, the table cleared of lunch plates and silverware. The six of them rested their elbows on the table, chins on their hands. They sipped coffee and listened to the story of the woman and her husband. Sunlight shone on her through the big front window of the restaurant, and she smiled while she remembered. "He was a friend of someone I had gone to school with at (school whose name I did not catch). Not that I was trying to catch the name. I'm trained not to listen. Just pour the coffee and move along, but sometimes things stick out. "We just had so much in common. We were so compatible. Our backgrounds were almost identical. It was very natural for us to marry."

That is lovely, said the voice in my head, though I knew I should not have been eavesdropping, *the idea of having so much in common, to be settled with someone without having to wade around in the shit, feeling blindly for another something you can grab onto, for one more small, shiny, reasonable argument to stay together*. I tried not to think about it.

Remember when you met him? the voice said on our walk home. *Remember that first year? God, that was a fucking mess.* It was my fault. I instigated the whole thing, that first night, that night that lasted a year, the world's longest one night stand. It was December. I blindsided that songwriter with arrant seduction when he tossed a cigarette from behind his microphone. It had been perched in his lips while he sang. Smoke drifted to his squinting eyes and he coolly tossed it away. It rolled toward me where I sat with Bro, and came to rest on the wood floor in front of me. I could have stubbed it with the toe of my boot. That would have been a thing to do. Instead, I leaned forward and retrieved it as casually as he had cast it off, brought it to my mouth and inhaled while he watched. He didn't miss a beat, just raised his eyebrows in the middle of his lyric. *Ohhhhh boy*, said Bro, and stood up to get himself a drink. Indeed.

The songwriter woke the next day in an empty house, no furnishings or books or records or photos to clue him in to who I really might be. I was gone. Two days later, a voice on the phone; he'd tracked me down: "I've got this face in my head, I can't get rid of it. . . . I was thinking of coming to town tomorrow." *Ohhhhh boy,* said the voice in my head, and I stood up to get myself a drink. Indeed.

And so it was for the next year. The songwriter would come to town, carrying with him a small black duffle bag that rested near the front door. The house began to transform around it. I ripped out flooring, replaced cabinets, painted, bought some furniture. I scored a free piano. In the early mornings, the songwriter wrote songs on the piano, then went back to bed. The kids playfully plonked away on it in the afternoons, hours after the songwriter had taken his black bag and driven 84 miles back home, back to the hometown I'd later share with him and where we'd fill a house with two more children and where we'd open a tiny diner whose stories would someday fill a book. Many times that year he took his black bag and seemed to be leaving for good. Many times I wanted him to. We were incompatible. Nothing in common. It wasn't ever supposed to last a year. He kept finding a reason to come back. I kept finding a reason to ask him to, or to at least open the door when he did.

One day the songwriter was gone. I don't remember the reason, but he was gone. Really gone. It was December again. *Oh shit. Shitshitshitshitshit.* My first broken heart. I had no idea. All these years, all the breakups, even a failed marriage . . . I had no idea it could hurt this much. I buried myself in work and taking care of the kids and getting ready for Christmas. At night, while they slept, I cleaned the house. I washed baseboards and dusted blinds and scrubbed the dark corners of the brand new cabinets while Ricki Lee Jones echoed off the hardwood floors of the kitchen. *Fuck him,* I sobbed quietly, pulling my mascara-stained tank top over my face and sinking into my kitchen floor. Then I'd grip my sponge with weak resolution and clean until I could sleep. I'd wake a few hours later, sip tea until it was time to get the kids up. I caught a glimpse of myself one of those nights, in the mirror I'd hung by the front door. I looked . . . *real.* It was like someone had peeled me, stripped the bark right off. There was something under my skin that I hadn't seen before. I was finally exposed.

That's how he found me just before the new year: clutching a cleaning rag in the middle of the night. I didn't ask why he came back. The black bag didn't sit by the front door after that. Soon it was flattened and empty under the bed and, unless the songwriter was touring, its contents hung loosely in the upstairs closet.

My father was concerned. Quite. I sat in my parents' living room and told him the truth. *Dad, I've waited my whole life to feel this way.* My parents, once incompatible people who successfully navigated—and sometimes forcibly hacked through—fifty years of marriage, nodded their quiet understanding, then wished us well. I had no idea what I was doing. I like to imagine they laughed at me when I drove away, and that they knew exactly what I was heading into.

The songwriter pops in the diner to fill up his coffee thermos almost every day. I like to watch him hop around behind the counter, trying to stay out of the way as he allows himself to be bounced around by this place. I smile, remembering . . . everyone was so worried about *me,* no one thought to prepare the poor guy for what *he* was getting into.

Lady Bird

The diner was named as homage to Lady Bird Johnson, a badass disguised as a Texas politician's wife. A First Lady who was widely noted for things like lemon cake and other mid-century housewifely achievements, she immersed herself in policy and sponsored a bill, the National Highway Beautification Act (Lady Bird's Law), which passed in September of 1965. While her husband was escalating America's involvement in Vietnam, anti-establishment culture in America was gaining momentum, and the Civil Rights Movement was finally getting the attention of Washington in the form of the Voting Rights Act, Lady Bird Johnson wanted folks to be able to see flowers and grass and trees while they were getting from here to there. And she got them.

She believed in changing the landscape. She believed that blight had unquantified fallout.

She believed that beauty had far-reaching consequences. She advocated for the arts, for early childhood education in Head Start, and she brought environmentalism into a spotlight that would have made Thoreau beam with pride. Lady Bird Johnson believed in nature, in patience, and in the power of minute detail. She was a true conservationist in pearls and coiffed hair.

Her diary entry dated Saturday, July 17, 1965, details that she was entertaining two couples (of her husband's invitation) as guests at Camp David for the weekend: "The John Steinbecks and the Billy Grahams."

Can you even imagine . . .?! Total badass.

I've been asked hundreds of times how I came to choose this name and I generally reply that I was invoking a philosophy that I hoped would guide us. I believe in the power of small things, and that no matter how callous someone may seem, we are all porous enough to be affected by what we see around us. I never want us to overlook the minutiae that could make or break someone's day. Every member of the staff has received at minimum one speech from me about how noble this work is, how intimate. Our job is to nourish. We won't ever see how far the ripples travel but every effort we make matters, never mind how small. In fact, I prattle, the smallest efforts are often the ones that reach farthest. Always look for a tiny thing that requires barely any effort, something really small like fixing a wobbly table or running after someone with their forgotten leftovers.

Imagine that we have, with that small action, cast a ripple that will travel a greater distance than we'll ever see, down highways lined with wildflowers and out and out and out into the world.

Eula

The day she was born I'd ridden my bike to work for the opening day of what would end up being my favorite job ever-ever-ever, a bright and cheerful brunch cafe in Manhattan, Kansas, where I worked alongside some of my best friends ever-ever-ever. When she was tiny I swaddled her in a sling with me while I waited tables there. It wasn't much different working with a baby strapped outside my belly than it had been when she was cocooned within it. We made really good tips. When she got too big for that she stayed home with her dad, propped in a nest of blankets and pillows while he wrote songs for only her. She's always been agreeable, this child, and the only person I know who is as kind as my mother. She is the third of four kids, and prone to seek escape from the chaos of a full house rather than lean into it as her little sister does. She reads and reads and reads, a book a day if she's not called to some other task. She wants to be an author, to bring everyone with her into the worlds she creates.

She started kindergarten a week after we opened Ladybird and I disappeared into the complete immersion of trying to get the busincss off the ground. After school she would come to the diner to see me. I'd bring her ice cream with sprinkles and she'd tell me about her day, what she'd learned, who she sat with at lunch, what they played at recess. Many days I was too busy or there was some sort of trouble that stole my attention from her and I promised her, promised myself, that it wouldn't always be like this.

Over the next few years there were lots of days I was gone before she woke up and not home again until after she'd gone to bed, days I missed every single moment with her and I'd sink into memories of her curled in a sling while I took orders and bussed tables, her tiny head barely visible under wraps of soft cotton. And I hoped that I'd done enough in those early years when I carried her everywhere that she could forgive me for these ones.

I grew up in the ether of second wave feminism, guided by an anthem that I could have it all. We'd come a long way, baby. My own mother spent her career changing landscapes and transforming entire cultures within the departments and organizations she worked for. She's renowned for her success widening the lanes of access for women and People of Color in engineering. Small and gentle and entirely beautiful, with soft brown eyes and a wardrobe of pencil skirts and frilly blouses, she challenged the norms in that field. She bent mostly white, mostly male spaces into prisms, recruited folks who weren't white and male to join her in reshaping the inroads.

It explains a lot about my own philosophy that the ripple cast by my mom's dedication to her work is still making its way out and out and out into the world. But she didn't have it all. Cursed opportunity cost, we can't have it all. If we're *here*, we're not there; if we're *there*, we're not here. We strive for balance, we teeter, we fall off one or the other side of the beam for periods of time. We have panic attacks on our kitchen floors when the big city newspaper gives our diner a gushing review because we are already too busy and we can't possibly handle more traffic than we already have. Ope. That's just me? We come up for air.

I truly believe in my work just the way my mom did. I believe I am doing the best I can with whatever time and talent I have here, just as my mom did. None of that lessens the anguish at the loss of hours and days with our children. Conviction didn't make it easy for her and it doesn't make it easy for me.

This little one, my third, she was just five years old when we opened the diner and I know I am missing from enormous swaths of her life, just as my mom was from mine. I'll make my regrets known to her, just as my mom has done for me, and teach her absolutely every other thing my mom showed me.

Right now she's learning to sew. I'm showing her how the needle guides the top thread through the bobbin thread and they loop to form a stitch that's stronger than it would be with a single thread. If the tension is out of balance on one of the threads you have to stop the machine and make adjustments. If you don't stop, your seam won't hold and you'll be a tangled mess. She'll spend a lot of time troubleshooting and tinkering and occasionally tangling. I wouldn't spare her that even if I could. I'll show her everything my mom showed me, but her own untangling will teach her better than I can.

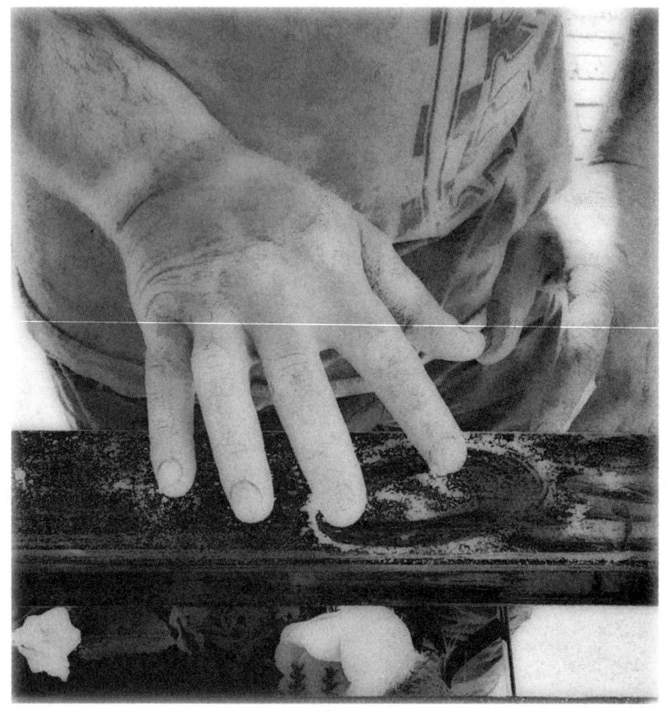

Galaxy

It starts as a bad day. Agitated. Just coffee, outside and away from everyone. They are all conspiring: the dentist, the assistant DA. He is going to sue them all. He knows there is poison in his face. He knows a lawyer. Nothing makes sense, and what is wrong with everybody. He lights the stub of a cigarette and I tell him he has to move off the patio to smoke it, a little worried that this makes me an enemy too, like the case worker and the others who don't understand him, but rules are rules. He sheepishly complies.

I don't imagine I understand the intricacies of his illness. I know that he is unstable. As long as he is in the zone of the boundaries we've set with regard to everyone's safety, he is welcome here. He doesn't have to act *normal* or *sane* or *like a grown up*. He says he's a wild patch in the garden, can't stay in the rows. I tell him dandelions are my favorite flower and leave him alone with his coffee and conspiracy theories.

It's busy today, and I hope there won't be trouble. I've heard he's had trouble at some other places in town. I know that the world sometimes feels like an assault, especially with so many strangers invading his perceived sanctuary, this little place where we pour him coffee and listen to his big ideas. But he spots the sidewalk chalk and begins to busy himself with a design on the railing of the patio. His motions are frenetic at first, angry even, but his intensity eventually yields to measured focus. Something like symmetry begins to emerge from what started as haphazard pounding of chalk against the rails. He slows down and deliberates, then grinds the chalk to dust, sprinkles it in swirling patterns along the rail, asks me to remind him what Saturn looks like. He uses the bubbles I leave out for kids to wash his work clean before beginning again.

The entire process takes several hours. He's so patient with his work. I could never be that patient, I think. Too conditioned to go fast and multi-task. I bring him a new basket of chalk, then kick myself because it's our last and I know he'll use it all up.

After a couple of hours he breaks for grits and hash browns. "Atta boy," I say, "carb load. That railing is not going to finish itself!" He resumes but takes frequent breaks now to come inside. He circles the dining room once or twice before winking at me and heading back out to his project. I think he must be getting a fresh perspective, stepping back from the details to get a broader look at it. It takes a long time to get it just right. It's a signature, an I-Was-Here that will wash away with the next rain. He's proud of it, and beams at me when he points out the block letters hidden in the pattern: *LADYBIRD DINER IS HEAVEN*. He has drawn a galaxy.

I smile at the metaphor of it, that with time and dust and concentration his frenzied, chaotic thoughts eventually found equilibrium and settled into something resembling a predictable orbit. Maybe today will be a good day? He says it will be. That it already is.

I make a note to stop for chalk and bubbles on my way in tomorrow morning.

Side Work

I was a waitress for 25 years before I opened Ladybird. Across those years I've polished and rolled silverware give or take 11,700 hours. That's about a year and a half of my life spent just on silverware.

The polishing and rolling of silverware at the end of a busy shift is a communally cathartic experience for a restaurant staff. Usually at an empty bar or table, we laugh about our day, casually divulge our mistakes, gossip, and polish away whatever water spots remain on the forks in preparation for the next shift. It's ceremonial, and necessary for the spiritual well being of a place. Also people don't like spotty silverware.

My dear friend Abby, with whom I've been polishing silverware off and on for pretty near 15 years, took this photo. There is no one better to sit with at the end of the day than Abby.

Look at your silverware the next time you're out to eat. It's possible and quite probable that a lifelong friendship was formed over your knife and fork.

Kianti

It's still dark when she gets to work, even on days when she's running a little behind. It's harder to get out the door in the cold months. So much work to bundle a baby for the ten-minute car ride downtown. Being first in means she can be first out, and that means half her afternoon and her whole evening are free for the baby. She likes the early shift anyway, setting things up before the diner gets busy so she knows it'll be done right. There may even be a couple of minutes to eat a quick breakfast before the rush. I know she doesn't get as much sleep as she needs, but she is no less friendly and hard working for it. She's first at the window to run hot food, first to chime a greeting across the room even when her hands are very busy and very full. *Good morning, find a seat where you're happy!* She checks up on the baby when she can scrape together 30 seconds for a quick text home. Busy days are best, those days when her shift ticks by in a blink. If she hurries she can catch the next bus, be on her way back to those squirmy, snuggly little arms and legs, those dimples, her true north. She remembers her breakfast still sitting in the back wait station and scrapes the cold eggs and hash browns into the trash on her way to check out.

Brianne

She only calls out maybe twice a year, on the days when she can't turn her head. Years of dance and waitressing have conditioned her to push through the pain. By mid-week she has already worked 40 hours between the diner and the studio. When she opened the studio six years ago she knew that she wasn't choosing easy, wasn't choosing comfort. The pace of her life and the sheer weight of what she bears would break most of us but her extra job at the diner means that there is more aid for kids who would not otherwise be able to afford lessons, more resources for her dancers at competitions. What she is creating there is changing the world for those kids. I've seen it. Expression, confidence, movement, courage, body positivity, so much strength. They literally lift each other up. In the dip before the lunch rush she grabs a quick bite, eating at the back table with her organizer open. On top of the classes she teaches there are costumes to select and competition trips to plan. She needs fuel and maybe a little more caffeine and definitely another go with the Bio Freeze to get through today. She needs a pick me up. But always, when she feels her energy wane, her dance family saves her. She knows that she can count on a moment of pure joy and pride in what they are creating to replenish all that is depleted. The little dance studio that could. She leaves her organizer in the wait station and gets back to work, keeping it all on track.

Here Come the Regulars

There are folks who have fallen in love with something about us that keeps them coming back regularly. They want us to win, and we rely on them. I'm not just speaking financially. They are an integral part of our culture. Regulars are to a small business what an extensive percussion section is to an orchestra. They bring their own quirks and add predictable beats in unique percussive tones, some high and jangly like tambourines or bells, others harmonious and low, humming way down on the register. Some are huge and hilarious personalities, cow bells and wood blocks commanding the rhythm for whatever amount of time they're in the building. It gets quiet when they leave.

I don't socialize with the regulars outside of work (not that I wouldn't. I just don't socialize with *anyone* outside of work), but friendships with regulars are some of my most treasured relationships.

When Jay comes in for breakfast I take as many opportunities as I can to fill his coffee so I can catch up with him, find out what he's working on, what marathon he's training for, prod him for a weather forecast. "It's a little early for Abba, don't you think?" I pop on some Dolly and he takes another refill. He's been a sounding board for my wildest ideas. I can always count on him for a perfunctory and unfiltered opinion on whatever I'm scheming. He tries every new item on the menu, tells me what works, what doesn't, then gives a wave of his hand and a *That's Just Me*. After we'd closed and started serving free lunches he stopped by with three nice bottles of wine, a pretty big deal because in those early days we didn't go anywhere, including the liquor store. The front window where he used to sit for a weekday morning breakfast is now piled with empty boxes to send groceries home to families. They're saving his seat.

Caitlin has been our most ardent supporter since

before we even opened. She was drawn in by the promise of homemade pie and has championed us in every endeavor since. Every fundraiser, every celebration, she's been there to support. She comes whether she feels right with the world or not. Sometimes she comes *because* she doesn't feel right with the world, to be in a place that will dependably wrap her up and welcome her with the sounds and flavors of a loving community. She invests her time in us, knows the staff by name, and has always made us feel like we matter. It's no small thing, feeling that we matter, that we couldn't just be any diner and it couldn't just be any pie.

There are easy to please regulars like Mac and Marcy, who always find a way to be satisfied with everything we do. Mac thanks the kitchen and hands them a tip after every meal. They find ways to be delighted even when we make mistakes. Some regulars might be pickier, harder to please, or require more attention than others.

None of that diminishes the beat. It becomes the beat. We sync with regulars in a way that feels natural, with little of the guesswork required for first-timers or less frequent guests. Real friendships form here, and the intimacy of providing nourishment is heightened by learning more about each other and staying in time.

In any case it's a real timesaver to know what someone wants to drink without asking, and also nice to further cement a sense of belonging every time we top off a drink.

Sean

He had his first seizure the week after he graduated high school. At his first appointment they told him the survival rates for epilepsy were lower than those of breast cancer. Processing that, he only knew that breast cancer was serious enough to have a whole month named for it, so where did that leave him? Over the years he's learned to recognize the aura that precipitates a seizure. He tries his hardest to keep himself safe; strives to maintain the balance of working full time and caring for his daughter while trying not to over-work and exhaust himself. His steady, relaxed energy is a gentle contrast to the intensity that often prevails in a busy kitchen. He keeps his movements even and deliberate. His cheerful baritone call of "hot food" from the window is always patient. He, more than anyone, understands that everyone is doing their best. Despite medication, his seizures have increased in frequency and severity. He's picking up a few extra hours this week. This is the last pay period before his surgery later this month. That thought scares him for a host of reasons, but he smiles when he tells me that at his last appointment he met a man who'd had the responsive neurostimulation implant. He says the scar was barely noticeable.

Sadee

When she took the man his food outside, the oatmeal he'd ordered and then left on the counter, he refused it. He insisted it was poison, told her he was getting out of town today, it's not safe here, everything has gone to hell. She let him finish what he had to say, acknowledged his alarm, then came back inside rattled and drenched in his panic. I told her he'd been trying to have a good day when he'd ordered. It didn't work out today, but it's something we can all grab onto, the trying. Her hyper-empathy is not something she can control, so I hope it's helpful to redirect it. I'd be lying if I said it doesn't make her a damn good waitress. She absorbs all the hunger and thirst as if they were her own. Most kids her age need time to develop the observational skills required to be great at the job, but she sees everything.

Her challenge has never been how to become more aware but how to process all the input because nothing, *nothing,* gets by her. Seeing and feeling everything as she does means she works in a state of sensory overload much of the time. It's like standing on a beach, waves washing over her feet. She looks down and finds that she's buried in sand up to her ankles. She pulls herself free, takes deep breaths and presses through her shift. She never shuts down her connection to people's feelings, never turns away from the torrent of needs. She walks out into it over and over, freeing her feet as often as necessary. She reads me a quote she's turned into a mantra "feeling anxious doesn't change anything," and I think that must be right. It doesn't change the kindness in her voice, doesn't change the genuine warmth of her smile, doesn't change how hard she tries.

Bookstore 20/20

Sometimes even seasoned hospitality workers experience stress at a level that feels unconquerable. We don't like to talk about it, but every once in a while there is a moment of such intense anxiety, or unkindness flung mean-spiritedly from a guest, that pings us just right and tilts us alarmingly off course. You find yourself, head down, emitting quiet sobs while you enter sandwich modifications into the computer in back. You tell yourself to breathe, puffy faced, doing your best to make out the words on the screen, fighting against a vicious rip current of frustration and stress. No tomato . . . your shoulders heave . . . sub cheddar cheese. Stop crying. Pull it together, pull it together, pull it together. Every admonishment of yourself produces fatter, hotter tears. Every attempt at redirection clicks you one dangerous notch closer to full meltdown, and god help you if someone asks you if you're alright. *Oh noooooo,* you realize . . . *I'm broken as gravy on high heat.*

It's a bookstore 20/20. Twenty minutes, twenty bucks.

We are fortunate to have two beautifully tended local independent bookstores within a block of the diner. If we can get a broken employee into one of them before full meltdown eclipses all hope, the likelihood of a complete recovery is pretty solid. Furnished with a discreet assurance from your boss that your section will be covered, a folded $20 that she pressed into your hand, and an order not to come back for twenty minutes, you are sent down the block to find a book.

It's not about the book, of course. It's about the bookstore. Whether they're meticulously tended or stacked wherever there's space on the floor, the cocoon of a bookstore is magically transformative. Your instructions are to wander the shelves, gently touch the spines, breathe in the bookstore smell, find something to read later, but not too quickly. The clerk will help you, but not if you don't want them to. Bookstore clerks are notorious for their intuitive abilities.

What an incredible effort you find yourself standing among here. If words are seeds, a bookstore is the Garden of Versailles. Linger just a few minutes, you'll find yourself coming back together as the calm energy of the shop gently whisks you into composure. And so you'll go out different than you came in, finish your shift without tears, Oscar Wilde tucked into your bag when you head home.

The Quiet Game

He likes to pretend that he is hard of hearing, and we must pass notes back and forth to communicate. I know that he's not because plenty of times we talk just regularly. Having once been a child short on attention and long on imagination, I play along. He is not a child but his pleas for affection are persistent and unyielding, as mine once were. I'm not so far removed from those days that I have forgotten that to be invited into his make-believe world is to be trusted, even counted on, to make sense of situations that sometimes feel threatening or confounding for him. Or maybe it's just a way to fully secure my attention for a few minutes. I remember that need, too. Either way, it's easy enough to indulge. He passes me a note that says Merry Christmas and I instinctively retrieve a pen from the bun in my hair to write a reply but he waves his insistently. It's important that we share: the rumpled flyer he's written on, the pen, eye contact and smiles, a high five before we mouth goodbye, a harmonious moment in his imaginary world, where we pretend it's silent.

Ally

It's a lot to be The One. He didn't mean to be The One, didn't even want to be The One. Like in The Matrix when Morpheus is all 'you're the one' and Neo is all 'I'm not the one, no thank you, I'd really rather not be the one.' His brain can fit together all the pieces of the puzzle, process new information while merging it with existing information, make sense of a map with constantly shifting boundaries. He sees the entirety of the landscape, keeps the latitudes and longitudes proportional, solves for $f(x)$ a thousand times. If I'd known the first time I met him what I would someday subject him to, that shy kid with kind brown eyes helping his mom run drills with my daughter's soccer team, I would have apologized in advance. He's still as tender-hearted, yet on an average Saturday he'll push 6 or 7 hundred plates of food out of the kitchen with all the composure of someone who has been doing this work for decades. The way the tickets ring in sometimes feels like having air forced into his lungs with no chance to exhale. Wait, how did 5 servers manage to ring 7 tickets inside of 1 minute? He raises his eyebrows at me through the expo window, his mouth twisting into an acrid smile every bit as charming as his real smile, then plugs the new variables into an ever-expanding equation, calls over his shoulder for 12 easy and 6 medium, go ahead and gravy a half biscuit, that's 4 chicken fry all day . . . all day.

Sometimes on weekends his Nana brings him a white chocolate mocha from the coffee shop down the street. She is tiny, tiny, tiny and walks with small, careful steps through the busy dining room, often accompanied by his mom or dad. I love calling across the room to him *Ally, Nana is here!* He lights at the sight of her, comes out from behind the line to greet them. He's never too busy for his family, never not delighted to see them. Spontaneous visits from Nana rank as peak priority above anything else he's in the middle of, and the dozens of other things he's juggling shift down in the queue while he spends a few moments with her. From my place at the front door I can't hear them, just see his real smile and the jaunty bob of his head as he takes the coffee from her. A quick hug and then Nana turns to the door as he pops back into the kitchen and picks up where he left off, knowing which things can wait, and which can't.

Real Name

I'm running late this morning and he is already at the counter drinking coffee when I get to work. I wonder if he was already outside before Kianti unlocked the door, waiting to come in and get warm. He's introduced himself with three different names in the last two weeks and I'm not sure if he is all those people or if that's just a more interesting way to interact with strangers. Today he tells me another and qualifies it as his *real name*. He seems tired and says that he has been up all night working hard, hasn't slept for 30 hours. I don't pry for details. I only listen. He tells me he admires the way we treat people who don't have money. He wants to know how to start a business. He wants to help people, too. He has good ideas. He is clever and young, not much older than my own son. He tells me a little about his brother and it takes everything I have not to ask about his parents. It's really none of my business. My business is to fill his coffee and get him a hot meal. I am not a professional anything, not a doctor, not a therapist. I could do more harm than good if I pretended to know anything at all about *real names*. I don't. I can offer food and a warm place to sit, and I can imagine that somewhere this morning someone is aching for him and hoping that he has, at the very least, those things.

It's Been a Busy Sunday

Like, really busy. We're coming down the back side of it but there are still several groups waiting to be seated. A woman stands silently on the edge of the crowd near the door. I've promised her a seat at the counter as soon as it's available. There's a solo diner at Counter-1 just finishing up. I take the names of arriving guests who talk with each other or look at their phones and she waits, perfectly still, looking toward the back wall while the bustle whirs around her. I add another solo diner to the list, then another. Finally a third.

I first met her a couple months ago when she stood inside the diner with her back pressed against the front door, as close to out as she could be while still being in. She whispered to me that she'd been told she could get something to eat here. Yes, of course. I led her to a table.

She comes regularly now for lunch. I know that she prefers a table but will settle for a spot at the counter if no tables are available. Always, she stops just inside the door and unobtrusively waits to be greeted, looks past us, avoids our eyes until we gently initiate, *do you need something to eat today?* She wears long layers of muted colors and a backpack. Her posture is so unassuming, her voice so diminutive that she takes on the air of a small, shy child. She extends the menu above her face and squints at it in a way that makes me wonder if she might need reading glasses. Before I go further, I'll admit that apart from her lovely name, that is as much as I know about her. Our communication is concise and it seems unlikely we'll ever eclipse the threshold of what is required to complete the transaction. These limited observations will have to suffice as enough to build the story on, because this isn't so much a story about her as it is about commerce and community, who is included, and how.

Much as I wish that my values were unwavering, I find myself debating how to proceed. I have three paying customers waiting for solo seats at the counter behind one who does not have the ability to pay today and will most assuredly linger over a large meal, as she often does. The voices in my head hash it out as I bus tables. Counter-1 accepts a refill of coffee, buying me some time. Is it unfair to my staff and partners when I impose a longer wait time on a paying customer, in this case three of them, while we feed someone who can't pay? But I promised the seat to her. If I backpedal and ask her to wait until there's no one behind her I know that she'll agree. She would wait or maybe come back later, but what would that even sound like coming out of my mouth? . . .and with that thought the dilemma is over and the answer thunks firmly into place. I'll seat her first because of course I will.

Because it is impossible to untangle the relationship between commerce and community, I have to give each root of those branches an equal advantage at the well. If we're talking about healthy communities or healthy commerce we have to talk about exchange, right? I mean, the root word of commerce and the root word of community have to do with interplay and reciprocity, but commerce doesn't depend on any specific medium of exchange to have value.

Money is certainly not the most important thing we cycle through a community.

She doesn't have money, but we deal in a different sort of transaction. We give her something to eat in exchange for her (albeit mostly non-verbal) participation in our little community at the diner. A terrible business model, I'm aware, but it feels like something I can almost fold up and tuck into my pocket. I'm here for the ride.

I don't mean this to sound creepy, but I really enjoy the way she eats. There is no distraction from her attention to the meal. She very intentionally and patiently cuts small bites out of her stack of pancakes, her bacon and eggs. She lingers over the food we take extra time to make from scratch. Her deliberation communicates to me that she is here for more than just physical nourishment and since that is precisely the nature of our business I feel compensated in a way that I can't take to the bank.

So on a busy Sunday I forgo the opportunity to make more money faster. I honor my allegiance to multiple mediums of currency. Everyone gets fed and I take away . . . well, what exactly? How would one measure such a thing as the heart-swelling impact of the words *I was told I could get something to eat here*? I have spent the last 30 years feeding people and it has not been easy work. My knees and shoulders are shot. I dance on the edge of anxiety and occasionally tumble across it into all out panic attacks. Often my brain is so jammed with ideas and observations that when I try to untangle them I can't even settle on where to start, so I back out slowly hoping not to brush against any synapses that might be sleeping in there.

But this: *I was told I could get something to eat here* is a feeling I wish I could keep under glass to look at when I'm old because someday I am going to sit down and when that time comes I won't need knees but I will need this work to have mattered. I need our time away from our families to have been a good trade, and hopefully for our investment in community to earn interest for someone somewhere down the line.

Yes, yes of course you can get something to eat here.

Patio Weather

As a young woman agitates loudly to no one visible about nothing discernible, the man on the patio comments, "it's a shame, because she's pretty cute." As though beauty should correlate with wellness. As though our appearance should somehow mirror our mind's ability to make sense of our surroundings. As though a less attractive woman in crisis would be less of a shame. As though she has disappointed him by not being the whole package. I say, "I wonder what you mean by that."

He asks me to bring sweetener for his tea.

Micha Anne

She doesn't so much walk as she flows. With her, everything is fluid. She moves through all of it like water, through grates of trauma and transgression. She has rehearsed and rehearsed the choreography for occasions when she is misgendered, dead-named, confronted with invasive questions and violent insinuations, She slides through, swallows it all before it can swallow her. She regenerates with a 30 second dance party, Raspberry Beret, then grabs a coffee pot and tops off the whole room. She carries armfuls of breakfast, still singing, runs the bus tubs, always a kind word for the dishwashers and cooks, always. Seriously always. She could run the whole place without us but she calls us friend when she squeezes past, checking us with her hip and accentuating the slight central Kansas drawl for fun, *'scuse me fray-und.* Friend. This is the friend we all want to be. This bulletproof friend, always creating, always hustling, always picking up the slack, always moving through all of it, swirling and beautiful, commanding her truth. When the silverware is polished she finishes a can of beer and flows out the door, on the delta now where the banks widen, but she stays in the channel and moves with the clip of the current. Life has taught her to move quickly.

Mike

He likes making cream pies best. If you can't whisk all the lumps out you just strain the custard through a fine mesh sieve and it's like the lumps never existed at all. He likes to experiment with new flavors but favors the classics, those pies that people connect with, pies with resonance, time-traveler pies. He says someday he will remember how he spent the Trump years in a basement bakery, making pies and perfecting swanky cheesecakes. He listened to the Kavanaugh hearings while he worked. Long after I had to turn away, he stayed entrenched, passed on what was pertinent and spared me the parts he knew would sting. His empathy breeds anxiety that makes it hard to focus sometimes. If he could show them how to whisk policy into cohesion, strain off the lumps, cool it into something that could be sliced into equal pieces, it might not feel like he's standing at the end of the world some days. He lights at the mention of us hosting a benefit or contributing to a non-profit. *Up and at 'em, this is where we shine.* He leads the rally, files away the frustrations, attends to the work we have to do right here, up the stairs and down again a hundred times, no half measures, every effort provokes an effect somewhere beyond his field of vision. He researches the chemistry of cocoa powders and coconut milks, tweaks recipes to the left and to the right. He optimizes his impact where he can: smoother, silkier, fewer lumps. Keep stirring, we are getting there.

Morning After

The day after the 2016 presidential election the diner was packed, largely with women, some of them in tears. Dread and resolve mingled with coffee and eggs. The collective anxiety felt like something we had to part like heavy curtains all day, but there was comfort and consolation and then we all gathered ourselves, determined to stand with those most vulnerable in the coming siege. Determined to resist. I understand now that much of the dread we felt was not only because we feared the implications of disastrous policy, but also because we somehow intuitively knew that this man signified the tipping of a domino that would lead to each of us having to recall, rehash and relive past traumas, many of them buried deeply enough we hadn't thought of them in years. *No one will believe you. . . .*

Maybe a good amount of our fear was rooted in the subconscious premonition that our most well managed tactics of self-preservation were about to be annihilated. More than a quarter of the women in this country have been sexually assaulted. Most if not all of us have been subject to threats against our bodies in one form or another, persistent reminders that we are not safe: thousands of days speckled with overt aggressions and mild insinuations, frightening intrusions into our physical and spiritual space, admonishments to be careful not to get ourselves raped.

But life is for the living, so we have carefully arranged the more traumatic episodes, folded them neatly and flattened them out and tucked them away underneath the scented lining of our lingerie drawers. We've taped them to the wall behind the spices in our kitchen cupboards. We've sealed the details tightly in jars and hidden them on the top shelves of our closets, way in the back behind the baskets of forgotten pantyhose. We don't pull them out unless we absolutely need to, and then only once we've completed ritual breathing exercises and recitations that we have diligently honed over years of practice. We are cautious, so as not to become unraveled. *If you tell anyone it will be worse . . .*

I've watched one after another after another of my friends, friends with busy lives and gracious hearts, slip into an unexpected, unwelcome mode of recall upon being triggered by a national conversation about alleged sexual predators in positions of prominence and power. *You wanted this to happen . . .*

Our more scrambled memories are being reassembled absent of our intention, and the ones we've managed to process and dissociate from are re-associated with no notice, without our conscious effort, and it's scary as hell.

It's like someone came in and ransacked our closets and our drawers and now the ugliest moments in our lives are all over the floor like an unwanted heap of hideous, smelly laundry. "Super," we say to ourselves. "Thanks a lot, assholes. I'll just work that in between the grocery shopping and explaining polynomial functions." Then we hastily try to refold it all but the creases won't reveal themselves so it just sits there looking lumpy and we can't remember how we did it so well the last time. It might just have to sit like that a while until there is more time. Until we are ready to let go again.

Shannon

Many times over the last few months I've thought of her and felt a rush of gratitude that she has a baby to hold during the quarantine. Stay home orders fit just fine with a newborn. I love that it takes the pressure off her wanting to come back to work too soon. I always went back too soon. She waited tables until her body told her it was time to stop, to rest, to prepare for what was next. It wasn't an easy birth. She labored a long time. She was mangled and exhausted and radiant when I went to see her and meet her daughter. True to who she's always been, she highlighted what was wonderful, glossed over the pain. She's a natural.

I first met her outside the diner a week or so before we opened. She was galloping up the sidewalk in shorts and cowboy boots, calling my name from halfway down the block. She'd identified me by my polka dot dress and jelly jar of wine, my signature ensemble. I hired her on the spot. She's been with me since, and I've been with her, with a few notable absences. I say notable because I always feel it when she isn't around. Things dim in a way that I don't consciously perceive until she comes back, lending her high tones to the arrangement.

She is a remarkable combination of polite midwestern woman and fierce advocate for what is right. During a busy lunch when a man won't stop coming on to her, she kindly asks him to please just let her do her job, which is really just to get his order right and not screw up his bill. Those things are actually *harder to do* when she also has to juggle unwanted advances and the fragility of someone who feels rejected. He chides her that she needn't fear, that he is a police officer. "Wrong answer," she raises an expert eyebrow, "I've known too many cops." She politely refills his coffee as the couple at a nearby table howl their delight. When men tell her to smile she graciously explains that there are a million reasons she might not be smiling that have nothing at all to do with them. "Don't take it personally, maybe I'm just concentrating." Her smile is radiant and authentic, and not everyone earns it. Pity for them.

Her ease with setting boundaries is hard won. Her mother raised her to love herself wholly, but the world chipped and gnawed at the foundation of her self-awareness, the way it does. She patched the holes left by grief and trauma, fought to keep it from crumbling out from under her. She uses every tool she can get her hands on to mend herself, to patch her heart. Her heart wants to be light. She rejects artificial substitutes for real joy. The authenticity of her smile is nothing short of a testament to pure bravery. Over six years I've watched her nurture what her mother tended so well, allow life to make her wild and windswept, use the storms to deepen her roots. She's held fast. She'll teach her daughter to do the same.

Of course she will. She's a natural.

Amber

There are always a couple pairs of her shoes in the back wait station, tucked under the table where we roll silverware. She leaves the house early, gets home late, and there isn't ever time to change clothes in between her shifts at the diner and the dance classes she teaches at the studio she directs with her sister. She brings everything she needs for the day. The few times I've seen her perform I've been in awe of the raw emotion she pours out on stage. This is the truest version of herself, something compelled from her very marrow. Teaching young dancers to find and expose this much of themselves is a challenge, but it's something she can't imagine living without. She's been gifted with a wry, sarcastic wit that allows her to save the intensity for dance, and I'm grateful that she doesn't exhaust all that passion on cheeseburgers and pancakes. She makes the rounds through the dining room with such efficiency that she could do it in her sleep, and occasionally has. She takes wonderful care of the people and this place, keeps us all laughing with her hilarious observations, but the deepest her, the part that expels what I can only describe as *molten*, we have no claim to that. That part is reserved for the kids who need to find out what is in their own marrow. Before she goes, she refills the water bottle she promised herself she'd drink three of today, changes her shoes and then is off to change the world, one tiny dancer at a time.

Ilsa

She's up early even though it's the weekend. Everyone else is still asleep, but she finds me upstairs getting ready. I work a long day on Fridays and don't get home until after her bedtime, so on Saturday morning there is plenty to catch up on. A lot happens in a day when you're seven. She fills me in while I fix my hair into a bun and put on mascara—no eyeliner today, it's a bad idea with so little sleep—then she follows me downstairs and chatters while I make coffee. She shows me the gap where that stubborn baby tooth finally ceased tormenting her; then she remembers. She runs to her room and returns to present me, coffee in hand and pulling my keys from my bag, with two folded dollars from the tooth fairy. "You can have this so you don't have to go to work today!" I blink off the sting in my eyes and force myself to smile. She hasn't given up on me yet. She is an optimist to the core. It's how she wants to see the world, how she wants to see me, still hopeful that everything might fall in line with her good ideas.

She used to pick a different window to wave from every morning, calling instructions to me from the front door, "wave to me upstairs!" Then she'd run back in the house and get in position to watch me drive away, waving and blowing kisses. One morning, already distracted by work, I forgot to wave. I forgot. She would have been waving through the window like she always did, watching me in profile, watching me not see her. Watching me forget her as I backed out of the drive and into my long day away from her and if I live to be a hundred I'll never get that image out of my mind, never forgive myself. She doesn't play that game anymore and I know that is her way of seeing what she wants to see in me, of not setting herself up to be disappointed in me, of forgiving me. She doesn't mind sitting in a booth while we clean up, playing puzzles and waiting for her turn with me. Whatever our reality is in the moment, she finds a way to let it be enough, finds a way to see the best in me. When the others have gone she hops up and asks to help mop the floors, signaling the kickoff of our time. It is her turn.

We learned late in November of 2018 that she had lost most of the vision in her left eye. When we left that first appointment I drove her straight to Target, bought real dolls for the dollhouse a friend had just passed on to us. She'd been happy filling the rooms with her own imagination, but I felt suddenly insistent that she should have the real thing. The good stuff, too, not the knock off brand. I called my husband from outside of the car in the freezing parking lot while she delightedly unpackaged Calico Critters in her car seat. We were bewildered. She'd shown no obvious signs of impairment. She was learning on schedule, her brain cleverly redirecting and compensating for a loss that had surely been occurring for months if not years. All along we had misinterpreted the frequent knocks into door frames and bumps into the dresser by her bed as the unfortunate but entirely predictable side effect of a high energy five year old in a house with tight corners. The guilt at having missed what was happening was replaced quickly by an unyielding panic. What followed was a series of excruciating appointments, more questions than answers about her prognosis, and the revelation that the other eye, the good eye, is following suit. Her world . . . fogging over, closing in.

This has always been my favorite age. A whole world to explore, boundless curiosity, endless questions, tireless energy, everything is magical when you're seven. I've been nervous, inclined to want to quell that curiosity, to try to convince her not to explore outside the bounds of her shrinking field of vision. Undeterred, she has made it clear that she will move forward with or without us, so we might as well get on board.

She learned to ride her bike last year. I don't know if she'll ever be able to safely ride without us by her side, but this kid only has one direction to go, and that's forward. We'll work on it every day; try to slow down the loss in the good eye as long as possible, hopefully forever. So many questions. So few answers as yet. Some days determination is the only plan we get our hands around. Follow her lead, forgive, find a way to let it be enough.

Why Pie?

This whole place started with pie. Pie was and has remained the thing most commonly associated with Ladybird. Ironically, our black forest cake recipe was featured in a national publication last year, but we are allowed to run out of cake. Running out of pie is a nonstarter for most of our guests. They won't stay. What's so special about pie? And if it's so damn special why don't more restaurants serve it regularly? Short answer: it's a pain in the ass. That's especially true if one is going to make it in large quantities and still do it the right way, rolling and filling each one by hand. The truth is that I could bake 250 cookies in the time it takes to make one single apple pie. By the time I've made the dough, chilled it, rolled it, rested it, peeled and sliced the apples, filled, baked and cooled the pie, I've invested several hours into eight pieces of pie.

So why bother? Pie is never going to be as pretty as its more postured peers Cake or Tart. When roused from its nap on the cooling rack, a piece of pie will likely slump, undignified and oozing its filling while its once perfect crust slips out of alignment in rebellion at having been manhandled by a spatula. Pie is testy, its dough cantankerous (sometimes downright mean) in the hands of anyone who overlooks either the precise chemistry or the matronly patience to yield a pastry neither too flaky nor too firm. "Touch me," says the dough, "but not too much, and not there. Now back away, don't even look at me!"

And the fillings! Of a million combinations of fruit and custards, each has its own fussy notion about what kind of thickener it wants and at what ratio. Too much and it looks like your pie is wearing too-small pantyhose. Too little and it's in a muumuu. I've spent many years trying to refine my pies' wardrobes so that they each have their own perfectly fitted Ann Taylor pantsuit. There are good days and bad . . .

But even on a bad day, even when I've plated a piece of pie that I'm not particularly proud of (and a few that I've been downright embarrassed of), I can always count on people to taste the effort. I can't even take credit for what they're tasting. I'm only one of many pie bakers in their life, perhaps beginning with their own parents and grandparents, who spent more time than is reasonable in the kitchen making something that was going to be consumed in less than three minutes. They could have made instant pudding, and sometimes they did, but those times you'd hear them early in the morning, padding around the kitchen delicately on their tiptoes . . . and you'd hear the light *click-clack* of the sifter and then the *chunk-chunk* of the rolling pin on the counter . . . soon there would be the smell of warm butter and cinnamon . . . and then the most perfectly imperfect dessert would emerge from the oven, bubbling fruit through vented pastry, custard cooling and waiting to be topped with cream. It's the tremendous effort involved in creating something so ordinary that makes pie worthy of making, and of centering an entire business.

Pie fixes a lot of things. Pie doesn't fix everything, especially the really broken things. It's just here to remind you that you are loved and worthy of comfort.

Ladybird's coconut cream pie

Ingredients

1 13.5 oz can unsweeteed coconut milk
1 cup half & half
1/2 cup sugar
3 large egg yolks
1/4 cup cornstarch
1/4 tsp salt
1/2 cup unsweetened shredded coconut
1 Tbsp butter
3/4 tsp pure vanilla extract
1 pre-baked 9" pie shell using your favorite pie crust recipe

Instructions

1. In a 3qt. saucepan, heat coconut milk, half & half, salt and sugar over medium heat until scalded to 181 degrees.
2. In a mixing bowl, whisk egg yolks & corn starch until smooth.
3. Temper egg mixture by whisking a couple tablespoons of hot milk mixture at a time into yolk mixture until you have added about half the hot liquid.
4. Return contents of mixing bowl to saucepan with remaining hot milk and return pan to low heat, stirring constantly until custard begins to simmer. Allow mixture to blurble for 60 seconds while stirring to keep the custard from scorching the bottom of the pan.
5. Using a fine mesh sieve, strain custard into mixing bowl.
6. Stir in butter, vanilla and coconut.
7. Pour hot custard immediately into your prebaked pie shell. Cover tightly with plastic wrap. Chill 4 hours or overnight.
8. Before serving, top with whipped cream and toasted coconut flakes.

Top with: 6 ounces heavy whipping cream whipped with 1 Tbsp sugar. Sprinkle with 1/2 cup toasted coconut.

A note from Mike, who likes making custard pies best:

Sometimes in pie, as in life, seemingly small things escape our notice until disaster strikes, forcing us down a rabbit hole we never knew existed. When our tried and true coconut milk was no longer available to be (oh so conveniently) delivered because we had changed food delivery companies, we thought little of switching to another brand for making our most famous and beloved pie: Coconut Cream.

The custard, which is supposed to be silky and smooth while remaining stable and firm, was a sloppy mess. I was aghast, agog, a-everything. I couldn't figure out why every single coconut cream pie turned into a swampy slough of not-pie. We were tossing pies out after serving only a slice or two, as great slabs of custard were calving from the pie like icebergs from a glacier. I thought it was me. My fault, my inad-

equacy, my inexperience, my unworthiness *to hold the secrets of this most hallowed of pies: The Ladybird Diner Coconut Cream. A cascading series of failures led me to an extensive period of research on the complexities of coconut milk.*

Turns out not all coconut milks are created equal, and their origins are all a little opaque. Purchasing the same brand won't necessarily guarantee that it'll consistently be made from the same coconuts, or grown on the same plantation. These food production corporations are massive and get their raw materials where they can, when they can. Did I mention THERE ARE THIRTEEN UNIQUE VARIETIES OF COCONUTS?

I discovered the brand we'd switched to contained more than just coconut solids and water, but also an emulsifier. Xanthan gum, guar gum, carrageenan, it doesn't matter; if your coconut milk has an emulsifier in it, you should use it to make a perfectly lovely curry. When making coconut custard, look for two ingredients on your coconut milk label, and two ingredients only: coconut solids and water. We like Aroy-D and Chaokoh brands, but you can try different ones and see which has the flavor that really works for you.

We find that the best place to shop for coconut milk is at our local Asian markets. We love supporting them, and they always have a great variety. If you find a Thai-owned market, like we have here in Lawrence, you are likely in very good hands. Our friend Nancy at J&V Oriental Market orders cases and cases of coconut milk for us, over and above what she would normally order for her shop, and we love her for it. Please support her business if you are in the neighborhood.

Thank you. Mike

James

This is his first restaurant job. In his other life he teaches English and writes and writes and rewrites. Backspace, copy & paste, shift the narrative, find another perspective. He might take a break when he's stuck but he makes it a goal to write at least 1000 words a day. In his life at the diner there is not much time to pause for reflection and there's certainly no such thing as a rewrite. There is no backspace on a Friday night when your whole section fills up and your boss is in her 11th hour of work and is starting to feel testy. No cutting and pasting to make sure we prepped enough potatoes for this shift. The only direction is forward and the cursor advances whether or not we are actively guiding the story. Losing our place on the page sometimes is inevitable. I say a dozen times a day *we move forward,* and we jump back into the passage wherever we can and pick up the narrative from there. We wrestle control back from chaos and guide the rest of the story to a tidy conclusion, something that knits itself into tomorrow's plot. In this way, I suppose, what we do here can only make us better writers. He and I have in common that we find some measure of currency in the rhythm of words. Whether we are consuming or producing them, we find nourishment there. He'll earn his MFA in creative writing in a couple years. Words and stories will be his whole life, and woven into that education will be these experiences of diner life, of learning to trust himself, of guiding a story that always moves forward.

Rebecca

She learned at her last job that inequity in the workplace is sometimes a wily little thing masquerading as normalcy. It's not always blatant or something that everyone recognizes for exactly what it is. Nor is it necessarily cloaked insidiously out of sight. It sometimes just shamelessly parades itself in broad daylight, looking entirely ordinary, masked as corporate policy. Stepping away from a corporate management position into full time waitressing may not sound like a step up, but taking control of her schedule and being awarded full credit for her efforts feels like an improvement. Her easy going nature and a killer instinct to think quickly on her feet ensure that her name is one her coworkers look for on the schedule, then fist pump the air upon seeing they get to work with her. I get it. I feel better when she's in the building, too. But there is a fundamental risk in employing someone who works this doggedly without complaint. She's a wheel that never squeaks and her ethic is so rock solid that she will pour into the organization without telling me when her own reservoir is depleted. She's so accustomed to prioritizing other people's needs that she is often inclined to table her own for later. Later she'll read that book. Later she'll eat. Later she'll sleep. Later, later she'll think about herself. My kids and I had a funny conversation about grading scales and how 'E' is for Exceeding Expectations and one of them was like "why would anyone want to do that?" and another was like "why would anyone NOT want to do that?" and the simple answer, I suppose, is that some people are just wired that way. I thought of her. She is a warrior that I, as a leader or boss or what-have-you, need to adjust my antennae for in a different way, because she is inclined to shoulder more than her share of the workload, to quietly exceed my expectations. It would be easy to abuse the privilege of working with her and it could look entirely ordinary. But the world needs her energy, this expectation exceeder. I will do my damndest to protect her for you.

Sit With Me

Sometimes when I don't see him for a while I find myself driving slowly downtown after work, scanning the sidewalks and doorways. He doesn't really have a usual spot, but seems to migrate along the main strip, maybe looking for a sunny spot on a chilly day, or a shady one when it's hot. Or maybe he's looking for a place he won't be bothered too often by the ones he calls the others. He doesn't like community shelters.

Too many people there, too many problems, he says.

When we first met he said he wouldn't be in town long, that he had inherited land in Nevada, no, Arizona, and was just saving up to get out there. An uncle left it for him. It was so cold that day, and I imagined him on a ranch in the warmth of the west, far from the soggy north wind that punished the few pedestrians along Massachusetts Street and swirled malevolently into the doorway where we sat.

Over coffee he told me about the farmland an old friend left him in Oklahoma. Just saving up to get there. Someone in Michigan or Minnesota left him several hundred thousand dollars. He was going there to claim it in the spring. That was nearly five years ago. He doesn't visit the diner as often when the weather is nice, but with the coming cold I'll get to see more of him and spend less time driving the direction opposite of home when I leave work, hoping to catch a glimpse of him.

When he comes in to warm up at the counter he argues with someone the rest of us can't see. That's not to say the conversations aren't real, for they most certainly are. Quietly animated, speaking sharply under his breath, hands gesturing to accentuate his point, his irritation grows but instantly dissolves upon eye contact. "How ya been, honey? How's business?" He puts his hand on top of mine to signal that he would like me to stay and talk awhile. It is a gentle, friendly gesture that doesn't make me feel uneasy for the reasons one might imagine. I'm just so much more comfortable in motion. It's hard to slow down, the fear being of course that a downshift at the wrong moment could cause the whole transmission to drop out and strand me in place.

I force myself to sit on the stool next to him, concede to stillness while the diner clatters and chimes around us, knowing that as soon as I get up he'll resume the quarrel I interrupted when I set his lunch down.

Briefly I am reminded of my oldest daughter at age two or so, sitting on the floor surrounded by toys, petitioning me to join her: "sit-a-me! sit-a-me!!" Sit with me. Just be here with me. Such a simple request. So difficult to furnish when there's so much to do. I don't regret pushing off whatever task seemed important at the time in favor of piling Fisher Price little people onto a bus with her. I am sorry for any time I didn't. I'm sure there were many.

A few minutes of pleasant small talk now while his hand rests on mine. His lunch remains untouched while we talk. I have his full attention. It costs me nothing, and grants me plenty. These days the usual template of my life allows for few indulgences, and this brief reminder that there is more to the story than cheeseburgers and coffee refills is welcome. After a while, too itchy to stay in place any longer as I can see that table 2 needs a water refill, I stand to resume my more familiar pace. He finishes his lunch. Before he goes, a quick kiss on my cheek and a see-you-soon, and I hope it is soon and that the world is kind to him until then.

Not Drunk

The woman and I have an awkward and frustrating arrangement. She asks me to give her a drink; I offer a sandwich as consolation for my solid no. She knows, but pretends to forget, that I won't serve her a drink. "You don't have alcohol?" she implores.

"Oh I do, but I can't give it to you. How about a cheeseburger and fries?"

She'll concede to my inadequate offer, loudly protesting my poor judgment, "I'm not drunk!"

I say that's good.

Most of the time the arrangement is simple. She'll eat her burger, tell me that she'll be back with money. I'll say that's okay, that she can always get something to eat here. There's no shame in being hungry. She'll go, but not before informing me and anyone in earshot once more that she's not drunk. I don't mind our arrangement. It's not nearly as inconvenient for me as it is for her. I worry about her, wonder how long she's been this way, what she was like before, what happened, how hard it must be, wish I could offer more than a sandwich.

Today was like all the other times. I ordered her a burger, she went to use the restroom, calling back to me that she was not drunk. But today the burger sat on the table for too many minutes. *Damn it. Damn it, I swear to god if she's passed out in there . . .* I already knew she would be. We can't get her off the floor. A call to 911. Stay with her. Ask her if her stomach hurts. Is she turning colors, breathing normally, can you ask her if she has a history of heart condition . . .

She is calling for something. Or someone, maybe? A name I can't make out. Shannon tells her it's going to be okay. Together we are able to get her pants back on, clean up where she has soiled herself, preserve as much dignity as I can while one hand still holds the phone and the operator stays on the line with me until the first responders arrive. A dozen people fill the hallway, lined up to help. If they'd sent an army it wouldn't be enough, and we all know it. Such is alcoholism. Do we want to press charges for trespass? Of course not. Her burger is still on the table.

A kind man returns after they've taken her out, tells me that they're taking her to the hospital, thanks me for calling. I nearly cry at the thought that anyone wouldn't. I want to hug him, but I politely thank him for helping her, and find that I mean it completely, as completely as if she is one of my people. I don't even know her name. She's never told me. That's not part of our arrangement.

Shan and I clean the bathroom when they've

gone, sing an ode to bleach, and I think about the hospital staff who will attend to her and send strength to them. She's going to be pissed. I suppose that we shouldn't offer her cheeseburgers anymore, but catch the thought as it escapes and know that if she shows up tomorrow, our arrangement stands.

Everyone is someone to somebody. We don't survive infancy unless someone nurtures us at least long enough to learn to tie our shoes. Somewhere, I imagine, someone has had to let go of her in order to protect themselves from the damage of a day like this. But everyone is someone to somebody, and if all I have is a sandwich and the capacity to call for help when you need it, well then sister, it's all yours.

Macie

"Double check your receipt," she hears the woman say, "she seems a little dim." If it bothers her she doesn't show it. Because she is sweet, and more probably because she is young, her capability is in question. Because she is young, and more probably because she is sweet, she says nothing to correct the rude remark made carelessly while she was in earshot. Had it been me I might have pointed out that I may be stupid but I am not deaf. Not her. She carries on in her usual cheery way, clearing the table and calling a tuneful *thank you for coming in!* toward the front door as she bounces to the wait station with an armload of dirty dishes.

It's the end of the rush and I warm up the fancy coffee she stopped to get me on her way to work hours ago. She goes out of her way to make me happy, to make everyone happy. Not a weakness in our line of work. Some people are good at this job because they are fast and clever, and some people are good at this job because they find genuine enjoyment in helping other people find genuine enjoyment. She is all of those things.

She grew up in restaurant dining rooms and kitchens, climbing on sacks of flour stacked higher than she was tall, ditch days from school to go do the things other people do on weekends because a waitress's kid doesn't see much of her mom between Friday and Monday. She never complained, even in the late-night cocktailing years when we were five minutes late to school more often than not. Optimism governs her outlook; forgiveness comes without provocation. Middle children are such pleasers. It is unfair that her sweetness would be confused with incompetence but she knows she is not responsible for what other people think of her. She holds her thoughtfulness and capability with both hands, steady on her feet, bright as pure sunshine. Never, never dim.

Last year, her final year of high school, I received a call from an administrator at her school:

Hello, is this Mrs. Heriford? I'm calling to let you know that your daughter was called to the office today due to a report from a teacher that she was wearing distracting clothing. Her shorts were too short. I thought you should know. If it were my child I would want to know. . . .

I see. May I ask, what is your policy on the appropriate length of shorts? Oh, you don't have one? There isn't a guideline for ALL students to use based on the measurement of the shorts themselves? Just an arbitrary summation of how they make a particular staff member feel? So the exact same athletic shorts worn by dozens if not hundreds of girls with, let's say, thighs of a circumference some fewer inches is acceptable, just not her thighs? And you deemed it necessary to call her into the office to tell her that a staff member reported her clothing as *distracting*, although she has not actually violated any recorded code of dress; and you didn't have a follow up instruction like 'go home and change,' or 'don't wear that again?'

And when you use the word *distracting* may we infer that you were concerned that her exposed thighs were presenting a barrier to the education of young males who might (if they happen to look up from their phones) view her legs with distraction, all the while ignoring the barrier that you put in place by shaming her for showing those legs? For daring to wear the same athletic shorts that thin girls wear with impunity in the same classrooms? Let's be real, what you are really saying is that a girl with her body type should dress more modestly. Had she been so lucky as to inherit her father's slimmer frame rather than my curvy one, she might peacefully blend into the halls and classrooms without the scrutiny of staff interfering with her right to an education, literally cutting into her class time to make a point of humiliating her. Make no mistake, that is what happened today. You laid down a little wall, and I hoisted her over it.

She informed me of her visit to the office hours before your phone call, giving me ample time to craft for you a vicious dressing down, which

I spared you only because I knew it would not benefit her. Instead I sent her funny memes and expressed my undying belief in her ability as a brilliant, creative and energetic soul traveling through life in an adorably Rubenesque body that will take her anywhere she wills it, over hurdles of misogyny, through tunnels of self doubt, and far beyond the horizon presently in her sights.

I'll tell you the part you got right. I did want to know. I want to know every time someone undermines her education, her right to equal access, her place in the world. I surely want to know. And you should know that the conversations that follow in this house will bend toward progress on these and all fronts, with a wary eye to the ways in which institutionalized sexism has shaped the way you see my daughters, and all the ways you will try to force them into a mold for your own comfort. We have so much damage to undo. If her shorts help her run faster and kick higher and smash harder . . . she's going to need them.

Busy Sunday, Part Two

If I'm being honest, it's a bit of a nuisance to drive him home on Sunday afternoons. There is so much to clean up and there's still the order to get done for tomorrow's delivery. Dry food storage is bare, hardly more than a few onion skins on the floor. It's going to be a big order. By the time the last tables leave the dining room we look like a level 3 disaster zone. He dozes on the yellow bench in front of the pie case while he waits for me to make time to step away. Sleepy guy. When I find a stopping point he wheels his wagon around the block to the parking lot. Damn it, the wagon. I'm going to have to put the seats down. I slog down the alley to meet him. Everything feels like so much work on Sunday at 3:30.

We load the wagon and he plugs my phone into the audio jack, wags his finger at me and smiles. His favorite song right now is *End of the Line* by The Traveling Wilburys. By favorite I mean it's the only song we play in the car, ever. We listen on repeat and he tap tappy taps the glove box in time. *Well it's alllllll right, riding around in the breeze* . . . tap tappy tap. . . . Next to us at the stoplight a chocolate lab leans out the passenger window of a silver car, nosing at the air and squinting in rapture. *Well it's alllllll right, if you live the life you please* . . . tap tappy tap. . . . For thirty seconds I am sandwiched between two entirely contented beings *Well it's alllllll right, doing the best you can* . . . tap tappy tap . . . and I am deeply grateful that the buses don't run on Sunday because I would have missed this moment. *Well it's alllllll right, as long as you lend a hand.*

I listen to the song all the way back to work.

Tim

There are a few books I make a point to re-read every few years, knowing that I will comprehend them entirely differently. The words are the same, but the reader has changed. I can almost relive the sensations I had the last time I read the passages, like uncorking time. Time is such a funny, elastic part of the human experience, and I don't completely trust my relationship with it. I can't tell if this photo of us was taken five minutes or a hundred years ago. When I cock my head to one side I see that we are completely different people. Tilt it the other way and we are still the same, words on a page. There are more adequate ways to measure our friendship anyway.

How many eyebrows raised across crowded dining rooms, wordlessly communicating our shared bewilderment with the circumstances we find ourselves surrounded by? How many high fives in passing? How many times have I asked him if it is too early for wine, knowing I can rely on him to give me the answer I want to hear? How many way-out-of-his-way favors for me, covering for me, wrapping things up, gauging my exhaustion with an expert analysis of my eye makeup? How many arguments over which of us the cute guy at the counter is obviously here to see? Actually, not too many of those . . . our dissimilar taste in men has either tested or saved our relationship over the years. For however long it's been, since way back before we were who we are now, he's shown up for every moment that mattered, as he has done for so many. There are no lengths he won't go to for the people he loves. I am lucky to be among them.

Ryan

He drives 30 miles to get here, past the two story bungalows on the outskirts of his little town, past the Store-it-Safe and the Coin-Op Laundry and a few other businesses with first names on the markers: Somebody's Quilt Shop, So & So's Tax Service. Across the bridge over the railroad tracks the horizon expands, sudden and glorious. Tidy farmsteads lined by windbreaks, rolling prairie dotted with clusters of osage orange and red cedar, a wide sky bearing witness as he makes his way to work. Good thing there's a view. It's a long commute by Lawrence standards. He's never complained about making the drive. He's never complained about anything. His second day on the job I overheard him in the basement singing Fly Me to the Moon and knew I had a keeper, less because of the song choice than the way he was singing it. His voice has a graceful enthusiasm that buoys the rest of us, converts stress to oxygen. Even on days I know he's worn down he never stops singing. Any song, all the songs. Making cheeseburgers, singing. Grabbing more chili from the walk-in, singing. Mopping the floor, singing. I tell him he sounds like a Backstreet Boy and mean it as a sincere compliment. He laughs and I'm relieved I didn't insult him. He leans into the rock & roll I grew up with, music my dad loved and raised me on. He is draining the fryer and singing along to Sultans of Swing. I am rolling silverware and tearing up at the memory of my dad's long-ago advice to see Mark Knopfler live every time I had the chance. We agree that this song boasts one of the best guitar solos of all time ever. He finishes up, wishes us all a great evening, sings himself out the door and, I assume, the whole 30 miles home.

Ian

He tells me he's afraid I won't have much to write about him because he doesn't share interactions the way most of the staff does. He spends most of his day downstairs in the bakery, tucked away under the steady thumps of life traipsing across the floor above him. He can hear chairs scooting forward and back, catches a glimpse of the dining room on his way to and from the ovens upstairs, but for the most part he is safe from the pandemonium, biscuit emergencies notwithstanding.

I remember my life as a baker. Early mornings alone kneading bread, making éclairs and tarts, lots of talking to dough, coaxing it to behave, a pot of coffee consumed in solitude by the time anyone else arrived. The job was isolating, but never lonely. The cafe was always in full swing and the case already half empty when I left. I'd weave my way out with a loaf of day old rye tucked under my arm, through the dining room, past tiny little old ladies daintily eating sandwiches, students nibbling at scones over their laptops, children with frosting on their cheeks and fingers, the din of conversation and muted jazz breaking off abruptly when the door closed behind me.

When I decided to chase this dream of making lots of pie, and hand making each one, I knew that I would need a team of really special people to help me pull it off. It's a lot of work, a ridiculous amount of work, really. He drives farther than anyone on staff to get here each day. He has pastry talent way beyond what we generally exercise in this bakery. The gratification of the upstairs view, seeing scores of people each day enjoying a piece of properly made pie to celebrate or to cry over, to punctuate a moment with someone, is largely invisible to him. But he trusts and believes and has faith that his work matters up there among the scooting chairs and tromping footsteps. A legacy of efforts sliced into seven pieces and shared with a community, the way pie should be. This is perhaps the most crucial interaction of them all. This is what started it all. This is our signature. I look around the dining room. Nearly every guest has ordered or will order pie today, like every other day.

"Interactions . . .? You're everywhere."

Jassiem

He'd been working for months before he divulged his challenges to me. Past situations had steeled him for the possibility that he would be misunderstood. He tells me before his diagnosis, "it was bad." They thought he was cutting up, clowning, acting out willfully. "Things are better now." He smiles when he tells me that he feels like he fits in here. I try to describe how this place is like a wet on wet watercolor, we flow and blend in beautiful, unexpected ways and it looks like this whole collection of people was on purpose, a design someone set an intention to, but it all happens quite by accident. None of us knows it will work until it does, just like it did for him. *Out there you're you but in here we're us.*

The eagerness he showed in his first few shifts and the whole-hearted longing to do well that characterizes most kids in their first tender weeks at a job show no sign of dissipating. His persistence and concentration are every bit as evident as they were that first harried weekend when I threw him straight into the deep end of a game day Saturday. He gets to work early for his shifts, hopeful that the kitchen won't be too crazy to make him a little something to eat, but if we are busy he is ready to get started, ready to be here. I sneak cinnamon rolls to the back when he misses the window to grab food before his shift. Teenagers need fuel. I didn't realize until he told me about his Asperger's that his focus and attention to detail, the neatly stacked pyramids of perfectly rolled silverware, the care he takes to move thoughtfully through a crowded space, were not simply ambition to do the job well. This is the way he navigates the diner because this is the way he navigates everything. I see that he's found a way to carefully and diligently establish patterns of movement in a chaotic swirl of people and plates, almost as if this was on purpose, a design someone set an intention to.

Erin

When she responded to the ad I'd placed my first thought was that I was nowhere near worthy of her. Her work, her activism, advocacy, her writing, inspiring thousands, traveling to speak to rooms of people about trauma and empowerment, the books she's written sharing her own experiences with those things; she has inspired thousands. But how could I deny the rest of us the opportunity to work with her? Everything she does is centered in community and the strength of each of us. Every conversation with her is an education, usually hilarious, and we are all more empowered for them. I wonder how differently things might have gone in my early working years if I'd known someone like her. For more than my first decade waitressing I considered harassment from co-workers, managers and customers part of the job. This is, they often reminded me, what I signed up for. It's better if you play along, don't make things unpleasant, they've just had too much to drink, they're only words, it's only a pinch, a pat, a name, don't be such a snob, prude, bitch, so uptight. If you don't like it you can find a new job. Sometimes I did. Other times I didn't. Not until it was really too much. *Too much* is not fixed to a spot on the ground like a starting gate or a finish line but rather attaches itself to your own ankles like a weighty shadow, waiting for you to notice the resulting friction and resistance. An action I wouldn't tolerate or a duration of coercion I could no longer abide, a weariness, a wearing down, or a discoloration on my arm where someone's fingers interrupted the very flow of my blood as much as my workday. Too much *too much* finally led me to seek out spaces and bosses that allowed me to breathe more freely, exist more safely, do my work for the pure noble aim of the work itself. I can offer her at least this much. Everything we do here is centered in community as well.

Once a week she comes here to feel her feet move, to flirt with babies, to do the honest, noble work of just making people happy without all the harder stuff that comes from trying to help them dig out. When we're in here, it's easier to pretend we've already finished digging while we fill the coffees and laugh a lot and talk about the problems outside. She helps make sure they stay there.

Megan

At the center of our machine there stands a gear. She turns with steady regularity and powers all the other gears, her hands in constant motion making dough, weaving lattice, crimping edges.

From the nucleus where she stands working, a warmth radiates out into the rest of the building, out to the people who work and eat here, and out and out and out into the world with them when they go, like something radioactive. But the gear just turns and turns and she does not see the power she's generating nor all the transfers of energy that result, how far her meticulous, methodical efforts travel. By the time she comes upstairs only a scattering of customers remain. She sits at the counter and grabs a bite to eat, a few minutes to kill before her kids get out of school. She uses the time to catch up with the rest of the staff and, in keeping with the incredible mother she is, ask them detailed questions about what is going on with them. She knows about them because she listens to them and because she mothers this way, buckling herself in to what it feels like to be someone else. I especially like watching her talk to the teenagers. There's not a stage of childhood that isn't her favorite, but she understands that age so well:

the anxiousness, the excitement; she remembers what it's like to experience every emotion in its rawest form, how acrid the heartbreaks, how inflated the enthusiasm.

When it's time to go she heads off to her own family to plug into the gears there, turning and turning, always powering the machine.

Billy

February 2020: He has a new mustache and an old soul. He knows exactly where he wants to go from here. He tries every day to trust the process, to invest in future versions of himself, to see the world at zero altitude because someday he is going to fly over it all and he'll want to know what he's looking down upon. The people will look like ants but he'll see their stories scattered across the landscape. He wants things to be perfect but is learning to accept imperfection as its own form of beauty. Not everything is well organized and the world can be difficult to navigate but that is what co-pilots are for. He is learning to rely on the rest of us, to let go of the perfectionism that's driven him his whole young life. He is presently a fry cook in his mom's diner, but someday he is going to fly away from here. We will never stop waving goodbye, never listen to Donovan sing *Catch the Wind* without hearing his laugh.

August 2020: He's been sheltering in his own place. Since the diner closed and free lunches began I've been militant about keeping a tight quarantine circle in order to protect the folks we're serving, many of them vulnerable to illness and distrustful of healthcare. We can't become a point of transmission, and that has meant insulating ourselves. He lives in a looser bubble with two roommates and that has meant few invitations to dinner or hugs from his little sisters. Where once there was a seat at the table and a hot meal and a relentless barrage of chatter in his honor now there are tupperware containers left on the porch, lukewarm if he's lucky. I console myself that it's something, at least, that he's close enough to pop over and grab dinner from the porch, but I ache and ache to invite him inside where he belongs. *Where he belongs.* The thing that especially doesn't fit about life in quarantine is looking out the window at someone who belongs in. That is everyone, but especially him.

Soon he'll be gone, on his own course and flying off ours, and I hate that I wonder if it will be easier to know that he's too far away to hug, and that the reason he is not here is because he is there.

Promise me . . .

Promise me you'll come to dinner on Sundays, at least sometimes. Your absence at the table is such a void.

Promise me you'll never stop making music, even if it doesn't pay.

Promise me you fully understand that as an able-bodied young white man you hold the skeleton key that opens almost any door in the world as it exists in present terms.

Promise me you'll work to change that fact.

Promise that you'll listen to the voices of people who don't share your access, believe people when they say they are hurting, and cham-

pion their advancement. Be quiet when they're talking. Give them a copy of your key.

Promise me you'll be the guy who makes sure the drunk girl at the party gets somewhere safe.

Promise me you'll always hold the door open for the person behind you.

Promise me you'll never use your intellect to make someone else feel dumb. Being born smart is like being born pretty: you're free to use it as you please, but remember that it was a lucky roll of the dice and not some measure of virtue.

Promise me you'll surprise your little sisters after school once in a while and take them out for ice cream. You are a god to them. They are going to miss you so.

Promise me you know that I did my best. I made

all my best mistakes on you, and learned from each one how to be a better mom, a better person; every shortcoming you witnessed in me made me who I am today. I am immeasurably proud of you, of me, of us. Promise me you'll be as forgiving of your own mistakes as you have been with mine.

Now go get ‘em.

Composition

It seems like it should be unremarkable. It's just a little diner. Make the pies and cheeseburgers, keep the coffees full, clean up, double check the locks before I head home. But it is not static. It is hundreds of interactions a day and so there is, during the clearing of plates and refilling of coffee and sweeping of floors, always something to notice if I choose to. Sort of like wiping a film off my windshield. I don't always have the presence to do it but when I really pay attention I am amazed by the scope of the panorama across a day. So much to see. So many, many moments to tuck away in the little internal diary I keep. Notes from a tiny diner in a moderately sized town in the middle of America.

Once, I made a milkshake for a chemistry professor and thanked him to the point of his embarrassment for teaching chemistry. I awkwardly gushed that even if someone never grasps the material he teaches, the realization that there is something there to understand at all is still immeasurably valuable knowledge. Reactions, reciprocity, change of state. These are ideas that, even if we can't conquer the formulas (and I can't), generate curiosity and wonder, and inspire observance. I can see these reactions every day, all around me when I choose to zoom in.

The north wall of the diner is constructed of limestone block from a nearby shelf that formed during the Permian period. A shallow, moderately turbulent ocean advanced and receded 14 times across what is now the inner continent. You can count that in the stratigraphy of the shelf. The oceans left behind tiny marine carcasses, which settled and calcified to form the stones that comprise our wall and lots of other buildings here. The net result of 20 million years worth of chaotic oceanic activity roughly 280 million years ago is a nearby shelf of limestone only about as tall as my husband. And what composes the rock is billions upon billions of teeny tiny little lives (and a few big ones, which are fun to find) that settled on top of each other.

With the wall as my muse, when I choose to I can see the billions of very small moments in this diner that have settled as they passed to form something solid. There are some big ones that leave big impressions, but as exciting as the larger fossils are to find, they are a pretty slim percentage of the overall composition. Moments come, they churn around in the warm, moderately turbulent waters of a day, then they settle to the bottom.

I offer coffee to a man with smiley eyes and a cap like my dad wore. He looks up from his book and nods. The moment passes, small and sweet, to become part of something concrete. It is layered now alongside the echoes of the crew who helped open this place and everyone who has worked here since, grains of them still settling into permanence long after they've moved on to New York or D.C., like the tiny mollusks and foraminifera in the wall. The layers form whether or not anyone bothers to notice them as they come to rest.

It seems like it should be unremarkable, but the walls tell a different story.

Metamorphosis

Hanging from the tin tile ceiling are multi-colored pendant lights made from repurposed Pyrex bowls in patterns boasting unclever names like Snowflake Blue, Butterfly Gold and Autumn Harvest. These were probably separated from their sets decades ago and sat waiting for me to collect them for a few bucks at thrift stores and antique malls. Busy patterns of wallpaper samples in beveled frames lend pops of color to the stone wall. Kris Kristofferson smirks from a frame on the counter and a bumper sticker on the cash register urges *Listen to Bruce Springsteen.*

Glassware and coffee mugs share space with stories we've collected: photos of Lyle Lovett, ceramic lady head planters, a taxidermied belly-up armadillo that arrived in the mail a couple months after we'd opened. On opening the box I had puzzled at who would send us such a gift, then remembered that Solace and I had ordered it late one night when we were hanging pictures. We'd gotten into the wine, *"you know what would really tie this room together . . .?"*

Under a bison head draped in a victory blanket of silk sunflowers there is a photo of my dad, which I rehomed after his funeral service. It is the one thing I meticulously straighten when it shifts a few centimeters shy of center. I whisper, "Dad, you're crooked again," or "straighten up, Steve," as I gently nudge him into place. Most of the other fixtures are permitted some degree of rebellion.

The limestone wall on the north side of the diner stands stoic and steadfast in comparison to its southern counterpart, which is made of bricks in various stages of disrepair. I've plugged some of that wall's uglier injuries with apron strings. Others are covered with prints of Vonnegut quotes. Sand seeps unprovoked from the mortar and gathers on the floor. So it goes.

The emerging aesthetic evolved with time and weather, a collage of texture and color. Most days the room pulsed with a similar power clash of human energy such that no one noticed how obviously thrift-minded I've been with decor. Unseemly wrinkles on the self-upholstered sparkly booths melted away when they were occupied, and what we lacked in polish we tried to make up for with sincere efforts at inclusion and comfort. Plates over-ladled with gravy dripped on the expo line and staff shouted above music and laughed too loud. In an online review someone once described our service as "overtly liberal, peppered with a touch of communism." We'd never felt so *seen*. I don't think it was intended as a compliment but we were very proud. We printed the quote on our check presenters. We were, indeed, overtly liberal with portions and personality alike.

There have been many times during the sack lunch days that I forget to turn on the music or the lights, packing lunches quietly in the morning light of the big front windows. I don't play my Diner playlist. There are no cooks on the line to wince at my Mick Jagger impersonations. And I haven't run to the stereo with an ELO emergency since we closed. In busier times, the whole staff knew I was having a stressful moment within the first few bars of Mr. Blue Sky's piano chord intro plunking overhead, just a notch louder than whatever song I'd interrupted. By the first drum break some kind soul would pour me a tiny wine and in 4/4 time I'd shimmy off my irritation at whoever had grabbed my arm to check their place on the waitlist.

I haven't tried to recreate those vibes within the new restrictions, but I do feel kinship with the *us* that we used to be. What still matters most is the strength and wellbeing of our community, and that has meant shifting the focus onto the folks who need us most right now. All that we were looms outside the walls for now, waiting to be invited back in when it's safe.

My initial thought at the outset of our closure was that although it wasn't safe to bring everyone inside for a while, we still had the ability to feed those who needed nourishment. We had the capacity to have groceries delivered right to the back door and a patio to serve a decent meal to anyone who needed one. Neighbors with means made donations, which we turned into lunches for neighbors in need. Old regulars passed us contributions for new regulars. There were warm meals in those early, still chilly days, cold cut sandwiches and burgers and bratwurst through the summer.

We became a hub of community resource collection and distribution. We carried on this way for nearly five months and although many days I'd forget to turn on the lights or play music there was a lot about the new way that felt similar to me, the lady who once shaped the vision. Community, all its lovely and messy parts, has woven this tapestry. When it wasn't safe to do what we did in a group we split up and took to packing as many free lunches as we could with six hands and thousands of dollars donated from neighbors.

Our old way of doing business involved challenging our own ideas of who is included under the umbrella of community. When we use that word who are we thinking of? Who is invited in? Who is left out? What parts of the definition are porous? Where are the gaps? We are a small business in a smallish town. Our success is predicated on the health of our community. I need folks who want to eat here and folks who want to work here a lot more than they need me. Investment in the people of this town is an investment in the future of this business. I owe them everything.

The ways we've refined our vision and transformed our operation in the midst of a pandemic can be explained best as simple chemistry. With enough heat and pressure, limestone becomes marble. All the layers of what we were, all those moments upon moments now under intense pressure and not crumbling, but interlocking to form something stronger and smoother than what we were.

Pandemic

The dream was never static. Fires, floods in the basement, never not something to fix. A viral pandemic was unexpected, but the dream leaves room for the unforeseen, demands that we remember how to steer. Pivot. Rework the dream, adjust the model, crunch the numbers and crunch them again. Gosh it's hard to model a business with so many unknown variables. What will August look like? And November? The dream is now conjecture and patching a path with whatever is handy. My grandparents had a colony of cranky bees in the siding of their farmhouse that they counted as insulation. Sometimes what stings us will also keep us warm. Stir something of that old lesson into the model. Plan another month of sack lunches and grocery boxes with real butter. From a car outside someone hollers to me to *keep on keeping on* and that means something very different now than Before. I hear: move forward with a plan that may or may not be a disaster. The dream leaves room for that too.

Some days this time of year the sunrise is filtered by particles from pasture fires so that downtown appears to be wrapped in soft portrait studio lighting, as though the brick shops and little trees are getting a Glamour Shot at the mall. The unusual stillness would be peaceful if the cause wasn't so unsettling. By now the morning dance should be well under way, but only a few cars have driven past in the last hour. That composure is broken by a man sprinting up the sidewalk across the street, screaming at the sky so loudly that his cries roar into the front of the diner where I stand bagging lunches. I watch him kick over two newspaper stands and a trash can, then collapse, shoulders heaving from effort and distress. There is no one else on the street. From behind the window I am likely his only witness. He stands after a few minutes, barefoot and sobbing, and begins to put right what he's knocked over. A car swerves slowly around the trash can lid that has rolled into the street while I have a short conversation with myself about whether or not to help, about what kind of person knocks over trash cans and what kind of person, having done so, picks them up again.

You are not the falling apart, I hear myself telling a friend when she was panicked not long ago. *You are the coming back together. I will help you.* Mindful and keeping a safe distance, I fetch the trash can lid and walk it over. Someone scared him. He is terrified. Someone did something on purpose to scare him, he says, and he's sorry about the mess, so sorry. I don't have a safety net to offer for this sort of situation. I only have sandwiches. After we've tidied things I bring one out and he is, for the moment, consoled. A sack lunch and a witness are what's available for now. He comes back for another at lunchtime, this time in shoes.

Some of the folks who have come to count on us for lunch or an occasional box of groceries may not need us once the unemployment checks start rolling in, and I will be so glad for anyone who can ride out the next few weeks safely in their home with a full pantry. The socially distanced collective sighs relief each day we tick ourselves further away from the last time we were gathered in a potentially infectious situation, tucking ourselves deeper into quarantine, each day without a sore throat a triumph, no thanks to those pasture fires.

Others, many of whom I hadn't met until a couple weeks ago when everyone else went inside, won't have access to weekly benefits. Still others have no pantry at all. There's not much right now that doesn't feel frightening on some level for all of us, but I imagine adding nowhere to wash my hands to the list and my breath catches. I'd scream at the sky.

For now, for as long as we can, a sack lunch and a witness are what's available. We are not the falling apart.

Soup & Sandwiches

Channon made soup today, with ham and collards and chickpeas. I ate it from a paper cup while pacing the dining room and it was so good I wanted to cry. There are just three of us now, doing the work of many. We remind each other to eat every day. I struggle to pace the hours, get more done, take out the broken down boxes that have been stacking up. It seems like it's been months, not weeks, since we started this. Time is bending and stretching and then catapulting us forward and that doesn't feel like a favor. The soup centers me, slows things down for a minute. It's all I want to eat anymore, soup. I honestly don't know what I'd do if someone set a steak in front of me. I keep saying that soup and sandwiches will see us through this, and I'm pretty sure I believe it. Soup and sandwiches until I can hug my mom again; soup and sandwiches until I can let my son back in the house; soup and sandwiches until I wear mascara again; until I can be who I was and cultivate my life as I once did, with lots of contact.

Outside a man pulls the apples from two sack lunches and sets them on the rack and I rush to the door to scold him, *please take anything you touch*, feeling embarrassed for my lack of tact. The last day we were open a man started to sit at a dirty counter seat and felt so slighted by my inhospitable rebuke that he left. "You could have said that nicer . . ." I could have. But I didn't. I leapt like I was pulling a toddler back from stepping off the curb of a busy street. It felt that urgent. This apple situation feels urgent, too, but the man tells me we need to address the virus as a herd and leaves them on the rack. I quietly dispose of the tainted fruit with gloved hands once he's gone. I miss the herd, too, stranger. I want to invite people to eat without policing their hands, but I can't even watch TV without cringing at the high fives and hugs on the screen. You can't DO that! Television is not relaxing. Soup and sandwiches until I can catch up on Schitt's Creek; soup and sandwiches until I can come home without my husband eyeing me warily, wondering if this is the day I brought the virus home with me. I wash up and hope that we're helping, that everyone who grabbed a box of free pantry staples is one less hand on the keypad at the grocery store; that every sack lunch for someone who might not have had lunch today will quell their unease, that soup and sandwiches are going to see us through this.

This Will Have to Do

I came in early this morning to wait for the food delivery. No one else on the street except Dennis, trying to stay dry under the awnings and carrying his customary ample armloads of stuff. A baby doll, a tote, something long and pointy, a cushion he likes to sit on. He tells me he has a knot in his shoelace. It's not safe to let him step in out of the rain to fix his shoe so I put out the awning and set a chair underneath it for him. I work on his shoelace from outside the railing. A man spots us from down the block and asks if it is too early for a sack lunch. Can he have two?

I can't get the knot out of Dennis's shoe. The helplessness that's been building for several days comes down to this damn knot on the shoe of a funny little man who does not understand why I can't invite him in out of the rain for his tiny pancakes. I rig and tuck the lace so it won't bother him as much. This will have to do. I wash up, grab a few sack lunches for the small group that has now gathered, wash up again and then again for good measure before heading down to meet the delivery. I miss my heavy lifters. That's what I call them. *Can I get some heavy lifters?* No. No one here but me right now. My knee is being weird, so I focus on how grateful I am to have the capacity to purchase goods this way. In come cases and cases of cereal, bananas, milk and eggs. Rice and lentils, peanut butter and jam. Toilet paper for the people!

A makeshift pantry will be ready soon so the heavy lifters and other downtown folks who have been laid off will have a way to get free supplies. Everything is changing so quickly. Needs are building rapidly. All over town, everyone is working hard in their own capacity to meet those needs with as few hands on deck as possible. I wonder if everyone else misses high fives as much as I do. Stocking the shelves, my vision of putting together custom boxes for individual orders gives way to figuring out a system that is less romantic, more expeditious. There is little time for decorum. It feels like every minute needs to somehow count for two. We will do our best, as much as we can for as long as we can. This will have to do.

Sometime today the sun came out, and when I get home I see that the lilacs are beginning to bud. This never fails to make my heart soar. My kids are giggling and bouncing on the trampoline. Home school PE or just a normal lovely spring evening? I don't think my husband has made it past guitar lessons in their curriculum. That will do nicely, I think. This will have to do.

New Regulars

There is always a line waiting for us at 11:00 when we bring the lunches out. We hurry to finish loading the bags onto trays and roll them out to the patio. Cheeseburgers and chicken noodle soup today, pb&j for the few kids who somehow aren't sick of that yet. Once lunch is served we get to work putting together the day's pantry box distributions. This is a quieter, less harried time of day, and feels easier to control. Portioning the beans is my favorite, something I would have found immense joy in as a child. Such sonic and tactile pleasure in the *whir-click* of dried beans tumbling into a paper sack. I can look out through the window and wave at the people picking up lunches.

Every day, a group of regular sack lunchers eat in a cluster along the edge of a nearby planter Sometimes they argue loudly and make a scene and I really wish the lunch was enough to quench their restlessness, but it's not. When they are done they throw away their paper sacks and juice boxes in the city trash cans and move their kerfuffle somewhere else. It strikes me that though they don't always act as I wish they would, that small act of citizenry is something. The proper disposal of trash is a noteworthy act of community in itself. I am filling boxes with vegetables and cheese, milk and bread, sneaking in little boxes of Lucky Charms for kids while Lyle Lovett is on the stereo covering Townes van Zandt and I'm thinking about community and what that looks like now, and how that song moved from one set of lungs to another and lost nothing for its travels.

This is the way community works for us now, financing pantry boxes and sack lunches with donations made from neighbors who trust us to play the cover for other neighbors. Every dollar that has come in includes an unwritten copyright permission: here, I wrote this song, I trust you will play it well. I'm thankful for these songs to play, trying to stay in tune.

We are keeping the show going as best we can, doing as much as we can for as long as we can.

Shelter in Place

Shelter in place, in this place. Channon is making Creole stew with rice. Erin got a head start on prepping today's sacks yesterday so I have some extra time to make chocolate milk. It feels like a chocolate milk day, let's go with that. Yesterday all the lunches were gone in about 15 minutes and it felt like such a fail. Under normal circumstances it wouldn't, but under normal circumstances no one would walk up to the door to find empty racks where they'd hoped to find lunch. It used to be fun to run out of things, that hilariously cheerful staggered chorus of "86 coconut cream!" zigzagging from Amber to Becca to Sadee to Tim to Ally (who was just chiming in for fun) across the room and back again. We're a shouty and boisterous crew.

Now we don't celebrate the empty racks and we never, never shout. Instead we gently direct latecomers to other nearby resources or sometimes scramble to throw a few loose snacks into a bag that will have to do in a pinch. Shelter in place, pace ourselves. We resist the pull to do more, faster. We steady ourselves to make the most and the best of this. Just this once, don't go hard. Resources are finite. I don't know how long this needs to last. Shelter in place until . . . until whatever comes next. I don't know what we'll be in a month. Different than we are right now, surely, which is different than we were a month ago. Sheltering in place, in this place, means not standing still but not going faster than our means either.

We pivoted to this new normal so quickly, hardly downshifting on the turn. I am only now making sense of it five weeks later. The transition back will need to be more thoughtful. I have ideas to flesh out when it's time. It's not time yet. For now, shelter in place, in this place, make chocolate milk, and hold out hope that everyone who needs a lunch today will have one.

Channon

She's made almost every meal we've served since the sack lunch days began. Pastas loaded with broccoli and cheese, Shepherd's Pie, burgers, glazed pork and rice bowls, soup and sandwiches. A crash course in commissary meals, all prepped and ready to roll out at 11:00 on the dot. We don't like to keep folks waiting. Some of them had their last meal here yesterday at the same time. We didn't start with defined roles or anything close to a plan for how to pull this off. There wasn't time for strategy in those early days.

We closed on a Saturday evening and began offering free lunches the following Monday. It began simply: pb&j with some fruit and a cookie, most of the staff still on hand to help fill bags and organize product. Initially I thought we'd serve maybe 30 meals a day? We had decided not to cap how many meals anyone could take, nor attempt to gauge anyone's level of need, and not to police hunger in the middle of a pandemic. Within a week we'd upped our par to 200 and asked the rest of the staff to stay home per the advice of local health officials. We divided tasks between just three of us. We were so ragged those first weeks, I recall thinking it must be March 3,247th. I missed everyone, even people I didn't think I liked. Where is that woman who always flags me down when my hands are full? Is she okay? I barely recognized myself in this new function. Loss brings so much weight with it; we really should call it something else.

I sat at my kitchen table one late March evening,

buried in grief, while my girls made bright watercolor paintings all around me. On the stereo Elton John sang *Mona Lisas and Mad Hatters.* I slumped and sobbed. *I thank the lord there's people out there like you.* Channon had begun to cycle through our inventory, cranking out heartier and more nutritious lunches, and the folks lining up for them were so grateful, wrapped up in the care she took. Hope sprang thanks to her nourishment, and I felt the collective shift in people who knew that at least they'd have enough to eat today and tomorrow. Weeks passed. Donations came in and food went out of the diner. She navigated a constantly shifting supply landscape. What monster hoarded all the pickle relish?? Months passed. Fractures in our local and broader society began to present themselves unabashedly as gaping cavities of decay. She made thousands of meals as the world churned. There were days her body was so sore that she winced with each sheet tray lifted into and out of the oven. Other days the news bored into her like a rusty auger.

She chopped and stirred and portioned. Through the spread of a pandemic, through the escalation of a global uprising for civil rights, through hit after hit after hit she chopped and stirred and portioned and tended our corner of the world, fought for safety and for justice, provided ease and nourishment to as many people as possible, including me. *And I thank the lord for the people I have found. I thank the lord for the people I have fouuuuund.*

Erin joked that if she was going to be holed up at the end of the world with two women in a building full of food and she was glad it was us. We didn't plan well but we've fought hard, and every day our grasp exceeds our reach by truckloads.

The Lunch Ladies

On a Monday in late June, after we'd pulled in the lunch service, Erin went down to the park to stand with a protest led by three Black women. They'd organized a movement calling for the release of a young Black man who had been held in our county jail without conviction for years. Years. I finished tidying up and went to join her.

No surprise, we were both arrested. When a wall of law enforcement three deep marched up the block toward the protesters, we hurried to meet them, sat down in front of them, and were subsequently plucked off the front line of the surge of protesters and taken to jail to think about what we'd done for a few hours. I think the official charge was something like *BAD DIRECTIONS FOLLOWERS*. I'll give them that.

This is where white women tend not to show, Erin points out. We labor in our own circles to rearrange power dynamics in our favor, to secure our own safety and that of our kids. We grasp for progress, expose misogyny, wrest percentage points out of the wage gap, and tend not to watch where we step or listen to how our movements are deleterious to Women of Color.

It's not *not* dangerous, but showing up to position oneself between Black women's bodies and police is less dangerous, statistically speaking, for someone who looks like me: round, matronly, blonde, not at all physically intimidating. My arresting officers treated me gently. Erin is ten years younger, fitter and stronger than me. She looks a great deal less like Aunt Bea than I do. She experienced less consideration than I did. Many officers told me they were sorry, that they were just doing their jobs. No such apology was extended to Erin. The bias is not imagined. Lots of folks looked on as we were pulled up (that was me, Erin was dragged on her face) and zip tied in the middle of the street. Some applauded us, others jeered, some just watched as we were loaded into the back of the wagon. Whatever anyone's feelings were about that, I can't imagine surprise was one of them.

It shouldn't be a shock that the ladies who hand out free food every day might also lend our bodies and time to advocate for other forms of justice. Food security is a measure of justice. Putting our bodies between police and peaceful protesters is a measure of justice. It's possible to do all those things in a day and still make it home in time for dinner.

Jerry

Every day after lunch Jerry stands just outside the door, plays his harmonica and sings us a few bars of a song. He tries to keep his selections in line with the feels of the day. When we served Creole stew he sang *On The Bayou.* Sometimes it's Woody Guthrie or Stevie Wonder, his payment for lunch and quite possibly the sweetest tip we've ever received. Scratchy, slightly off key, it's what he has. When he told us that his old one didn't play all the notes, Erin bought him 2 new harmonicas, a G and a C. We weren't quite sure which he'd prefer because he doesn't always sing in the same key as the harp, so she got both. Friday he sang me a few verses of *I Can See Clearly Now,* swaying and smiling at me from the sunny sidewalk just beyond the patio rail. In truth, things are foggy right now and I can't see a clear way back to what we were . . . before.

Before, Ladybird was a swirling patchwork of color and movement, worn in the places it's been loved the most. We've never pretended to be polished or any sort of a tight ship. The thought of modifying this incredibly tiny diner with the sorts of measures required to mitigate the spread of a viral pandemic are silly to think about but I entertain the fantasies for a while. Servers and cooks in masks and plastic face shields. Space age plexiglass dining pods with aerosol hoses plumbed in to automatically disinfect every surface with a fog of sanitizer between guests. Extravagant hands-free delivery systems, conveyor belts parading lines of chicken fried steaks and pancakes like luggage. Human contact reduced to the barest minimum with ridiculous upgrades if those things could exist at all. Ours is an industry of single digit profit margins when we're running at full capacity, but even if such contraptions were available and we could afford them why would we want to?

Our work is centered in hugs and high fives, heads bent together laughing, peek-a-booing the babies and pushing in chairs for the grannies, millions of moments spent in closeness with one another beneath the overstory of a vibrant community exchange. Contact is not required, of course, but the sterility and loss of closeness feels unthinkably disconnective. Who even are we without those things? I keep hearing we're all in this together but lots of our regulars these days don't have consistent access to water and soap. We're not exactly in the same boat. Nothing about policing other folks' bodies and hygiene feels right, so who gets to come in and who is left out?

The notion of us returning to business as usual, even a modified usual, is beyond reach right now. However we adapt when it's time, the model will include Jerry and his tuneful tributes after lunch. There are some things I refuse to give up.

Toughest Customer

She appeared at the door on a sweltering July afternoon wearing layers of thick clothing many sizes too large. A jacket over a sweater, jeans so oversized she has to hold them up with one hand when she crosses the street. She is not good at crossing the street. She steps out between parked cars and meanders to the center line where she waits to cross the other lane; holding up her jeans with one hand as she takes several steps in one direction or another, confusing the drivers on both sides. New to town or new to this circumstance? I'm not sure. She is skittish and does not make eye contact when we speak. We call her our toughest customer.

Despite her shyness she haggles, and she is difficult to please. We go in circles over things like juice, or what fresh vegetables are available. Orange and yellow vegetables are on a list of foods so unacceptable that I must be an idiot to offer them. Many of my suggestions for foods that won't require refrigeration or reheating offend her, and she returns to the door several times a day hoping for a better outcome. I am trying to learn what counts as a successful transaction with her. I ask what she'd like—she asks what I have—I list what I have—she asks for something else. Back and forth until we flub the volley. We both look down. The floor is lava. No points for anyone.

Our miscommunications are so confounding that I feel a halo of static frustration buzzing over my head. I am certain she feels the same. Still, twenty minutes later she is back at the door for the third time in an hour and we finally settle on a bag of broccoli and cucumbers, grape juice and vanilla yogurt.

In the morning she is out front an hour before lunch service, watching me while I fill the bags and ice the drinks. She's not impatient, just observing. She stands with her forehead pressed against the glass of the front door and when I look up again her eyes are closed. She appears to be asleep on her feet. She is exhausted. Others begin lining up, frenetic and jovial, transforming the sidewalk into the closest thing we'll get to a carnival during this pandemic summer: a little precarious, rough and dusty, not at all unpleasant. By the time we wheel out the lunches she has disappeared.

She comes back after the crowd thins, crosses the street (badly) to the racks of lunches, which are now significantly depleted. She asks what items are no longer available, knowing she would have been first in line. She wants to know what she's been denied. She takes two sacks of egg salad sandwiches and juice with no complaint. That should feel like a win. It doesn't. Her lack of protestation feels hollow and I find myself troubled that she isn't giving me a hard time about the slim selection remaining. *Don't give up, don't give up. Stay and fight.* Serve the ball and I will volley. Fight about juice, fight about distasteful orange and yellow vegetables, fight about anything at all until you can fight for a pair of shoes that fit and a place you can sleep soundly. Fight for your right of way. Take up space, be unpleasant, but god damn it keep that ball in the air. The floor . . . the floor is lava.

Pride

Occasionally we get an email that someone didn't come to pick up their scheduled pantry box because their pride got in the way. I wish I could explain how much it means to be able to serve lunch and fill boxes of food for folks right now. How it's changed everything. How it's transformed my vision for what we will be moving forward, blending what we were in the Before Times and what we are now. How serving free lunches and packing groceries have buoyed my focus on every next right thing.

We took a week off to rest in July, having found ourselves near collapse from the pace and the weight the first three months. We came back feeling something like rejuvenated, or as close as we'll get right now. The world was still heavy but our commitment to steward our corner was in better repair after a week with our families. Channon had time to tootle about in her new place and she and Erin had a chance to just be, just *be* for a bit. I went hard in the garden, played with my babies, caught up with my husband over late night drinks on the porch, fleshed out the plan of what's next for Ladybird. On Monday at lunch service one of our regulars, a smiley man who keeps his belongings in a black trash bag, asked if we'd had a nice break. The question was steeped in such sincerity, like something you'd ask a friend who just got back from vacation. It was a well wish, a hope that we're cared for. What he has to trade for lunch is giving a damn. Priceless. We resumed pantry box distributions and I hoped anyone who'd hesitated before was able to feel a sense of pride that they're part of this, too. Pride is what makes the whole thing work. Pride fills the boxes, picks them up and shuttles them home to be made into meals. Pride nourishes the fight. Mine, yours, ours, all of us who give a damn.

Wobble

Is this the first time in 3 months that I've felt myself really wobble? Bars closing again. We're going the wrong way. Still neighbors being laid off, still lots of people needing lunches and groceries, still no way to offer anyone a good job in a way that ensures their safety. Even my best ideas about reopening are just that: notions, untested.

The last couple days I've begun to catch myself breathing too shallowly and I remind myself to inhale deeply, caution myself not to panic. Steady on. Keep packing lunches. Keep filling boxes. The truck will be here in a couple of minutes. Maybe if I reorganize the dry goods that now occupy the sparkly booths in the dining room something like clarity will present itself. I laugh out loud remembering all the times I barked at staff not to lean their pointy knees on the benches when they'd wipe the tables because it wears the vinyl out. Now the vinyl is dented and misshapen from being stacked with heavy cases of food. Priorities shift.

Maybe I can find better order in my thoughts if the potatoes and onions are tidy, if the cereals and pastas are stacked and arranged in rows. Or maybe it's just this and this still has to do for now. We said *as much as we can for as long as we can*. We can keep going, keep providing what we have access to for now. Anyway, my worst idea was probably that I thought I'd have a better one by now.

For now, for July, just keep going. Steady on.

Terrible Capitalist

When observing the behaviors of business owners in a capitalist economy before I became one myself, I gathered that I was supposed to make decisions in my own self-interest. View land, labor and capital as resources to produce something that I could sell. Sell as much of that thing as possible, then take the profits and either try to make more and sell more of the thing, or maybe make and sell another thing, or spend the money on myself, or some combination therein.

No one will argue that I am a good capitalist, or even a good business owner. We keep giving the money away. I have no desire to open a second location, EVER. A couple of times folks have asked about franchising Ladybird. *Let's see. You're going to need a buffalo head, some bass boat vinyl, a picture of my dad, a crumbly wall . . . oh, and you're going to give all the money away. Hey, friend, where are you going?*

I landed in the right town to be a terrible capitalist. The market here favors small business and there are several other terrible capitalists around. Some of them have been in business a long time. Competition? That's for corporations and is not a favored tactic of small main street markets. There is and has long been real cooperation among small businesses everywhere. If there is an enemy it is any logo that takes satisfaction in homogeny and would swallow us whole by the thousands like krill as it skims, feeding across local markets it doesn't even know exist.*

So what happens when a pandemic changes everything about the way commerce moves around a community? New restrictions on how businesses can operate safely have inspired collaboration among neighbors, merging of services, pairings between bars and restaurants, between cafes and boutiques, a true linking of arms as we trudge further into a receding economy. Among ourselves and within our communities, small business owners and staff coordinate, rally to buttress the strain on critical services like food and shelter, and cheer each other on. Where

*Please read *How to Resist Amazon and Why*, by Danny Caine, owner of Raven Bookstore in Lawrence, Kansas. You can find that at your local independent book retailer, or order it from ravenbookstore.com.

we used to swim without touching the bottom, many of us are now ankle deep in a muddy puddle, gripping ever tightly each passing week, trying to hold each other steady as we wait for the tide to come in. My god, none of us wants to be the last one standing.

An age of radical interdependence is underway. Small businesses, if we survive, will be among the best prepared to show the way. Our strength has always been symbiosis, and many of us have already found plenty of ways to successfully operate within a capitalist system without buying into the idea that competition is more essential than cooperation. We deal in forms of currency that never find their way to a bank bag. We know that individualism is not stronger than community. We've been working on economic herd immunity for years, and we've done it while paying our taxes. We've done it while striving to pay our employees an increasing living wage. We've done it while contributing to the boots-on-the-ground nonprofits that make essential connections between people and critical services. We've done it while advocating for justice within our own organizations and in our broader communities.

Ladybird started with a simple braid of commerce: a product, a market, a labor force. Over the years we've plaited in calls for support from the community to form a more elaborate model. When our staff talks about growth we don't bring spreadsheets to the conversation. We're specifically measuring the potential of our impact and consciously choosing to center community and heed calls for support whenever and wherever possible. Shareholders in this scenario are individuals and organizations who need bracing up. That's where the extra goes, and when there isn't any extra we put out a call, host a benefit, bake some extra pies.

Any measure we take which strengthens the

community around us is an investment in growth. We define our standard of success not by dollars retained but by resources shared. Our growth trajectory is centered in how well we're able to collaborate with and serve our larger community, beginning with the folks who work and eat at the diner but certainly not ending there. I don't want to be bigger, but I do want to do more.

This is where the pillars of capitalism finally come in handy: a.) sure, the goal is to amass wealth, but we can define that word any way we like; b.) division of labor increases output, so more of us are better; and c.) anything that yields growth more quickly adds value as a force multiplier. If the goal, *if growth*, is a wholly vibrant and healthy community, human rights for everyone is not only achievable but only a few exponential degrees away from being reality. If I were going to franchise anything, it would be that.

Last Post

DJ has been here nearly every day since we started free lunches. Today, learning that Channon made her mac and cheese, super cheesy and spiced the way she does, loaded with smoked pork and veggies, he does a little hop and fist pump and asks for another sack for later. "I'll tell you the truth," he says, "this is the only time I eat." Erin and I deflate a little, knowing that the well is about dried up here, and that it's time to regroup and make a new plan that will sustain free lunches a while longer.

It's harvest time. Stop everything and tend to a thing that can't wait, a thing that must be done right now. For years I've been dropping seeds along the way, and now it's time to gather whatever fruit has grown. With an eye to chilly months ahead we'll spend August mining our resources and collecting what we need to provide at least one good meal a day for our neighbors who need it, hopefully for the rest of the year, and throughout the winter season when a hot meal matters most. The last four months have exposed frailties I hadn't realized existed, and revealed surprising areas of strength. We are not as we were; we've shifted our priorities and narrowed our focus to serving those with the greatest need for food right now, *right now*. Right now is still happening, *right now* several months later, and soon right now will be cold.

August brings a step away from the diner, a harvesting, and hopefully bushels for September and beyond. I am already dreaming of warm, rich stews and hunks of cornbread with butter, and of little hops and fist pumps when we hand them out.

Afterword, August 2020

This collection of essays was cultivated over the span of our first six years in business. This is the harvest. It's a window into the evolution of Ladybird Diner, of what we were and how a pandemic changed everything and nothing about us. If you purchased this book, you've helped to fund meals for the community kitchen that we hope to maintain for the duration of our pandemic-related closure and as long as we're needed in that capacity. We're still us. Our mission hasn't changed, but the framework has. Lots of small businesses won't survive the economic fallout of this pandemic. Maybe we won't, either, but we will go down swinging if we go down. For us, that means doing as much as we can for as long as we can to support the community that has shaped the life of this tiny diner in the middle of the country.

About the Author

This is a weird page to write. I don't fancy myself an author. I am a diner owner. I didn't want to write an *About the Author* but the page count is off and I'm in a hurry to sell some copies of this book because people need food right now. I asked Erin to take this one and she said:

She's known for midwestern hospitality, creative comfort food and unapologetic feminist backbone. You can spot her by her tiny glass of cava, colorfully printed dress and in a hurry to whatever is next.

There's more to know, quite a lot that doesn't fit in this book, things that are not specific to life since Ladybird. I suppose the most important bit is that I try to see what's unique and real about the places and people near me. I seek metaphor over coincidence because it comforts me to think that some things are universal. I'm not sure what that's good for, but I wrote this book just in case.